A NEW HISTORY OF IRELAND

UNDER THE AUSPICES OF THE ROYAL IRISH ACADEMY

edited by

T. W. MOODY, F. X. MARTIN and F. J. BYRNE

ANCILLARY PUBLICATIONS I

MEDIEVAL IRELAND, *c.*1170-1495:
A BIBLIOGRAPHY OF SECONDARY WORKS

MEDIEVAL IRELAND
c. 1170-1495

A Bibliography of Secondary Works

by
P. W. A. ASPLIN

DUBLIN
ROYAL IRISH ACADEMY
1971

Set in 8 point and 10 point Monotype Times New Roman

Printed and made in the Republic of Ireland by
Leinster Leader Ltd., Naas

CONTENTS

PREFACE

This is the first of a projected series of publications ancillary to *A new history of Ireland*, a co-operative enterprise of some sixty-five scholars, which, under the auspices of the Royal Irish Academy, has been in progress since 1968. It is planned for completion by the end of 1973, and is to be published, in nine volumes, as soon as possible after that date. Meanwhile, the board of editors intend to publish bibliographical, statistical and other aids to study and research, both to facilitate and expedite work on the *New history* and also to assist the progress of Irish historical scholarship generally. Bibliography is a field in which the need for such aids is specially urgent, and we are happy to launch our series of Ancillary Publications with the present bibliography of medieval Ireland by a historical scholar who has been working on the subject for some years. We are confident that Mr Asplin's book will be of immediate value for the writers of the *New history* and will prove an indispensable guide to the historiography of medieval Ireland.

Mr Asplin is concerned only with printed secondary writing; while recording bibliographies and guides to sources, he does not include source materials, either manuscript or printed, as such. He draws selectively on publications dating from the early seventeenth century, and his book is specially useful for its wealth of articles that have appeared in periodicals during the past century. Attention should be drawn to the importance of his list of serial publications, which provides a conspectus, with full bibliographical details, of all the major publications in this category. Mr Asplin's identification of periods and subjects is also particularly helpful and suggestive.

We are grateful to him for the learning and the care he has devoted to this work and for his ready co-operation.

T. W. Moody
F. X. Martin
F. J. Byrne

INTRODUCTION

This bibliography had its origins in a much shorter compilation submitted in part fulfilment of the postgraduate Diploma in Librarianship at the University of Strathclyde in 1966. Subsequent development as a guide for the undergraduate, involving considerable changes in scope and emphasis, was encouraged by Professors J. Otway-Ruthven and J. F. Lydon of the University of Dublin, and was almost completed in 1969 when the work was adopted for publication by the board of editors of *A new history of Ireland*. This background accounts for certain discrepancies between the present work and the plan for the *New history* itself. In particular, 1495 has been adopted as a terminal date, following both existing standard histories of medieval Ireland, whereas the second volume of the *New history* will cover the period 1169-1534.

It should be emphasised that this is a bibliography of *secondary* works —a guide to primary sources is being edited for the Irish Manuscripts Commission by Dr J. F. Lydon. However, the more important published guides to sources have been listed here, and full bibliographical information has been given whenever a particular published source has been referred to in the notes. Local history as such has been omitted, although an attempt has been made to include local events of more than local significance and items on special topics which can be regarded as representative in the absence of comprehensive treatment for the country as a whole. Coverage of background and auxiliary subjects in sections X-XVIII, and to some extent social and economic history in section IX, should also be taken as representative. On the wider front, some older general works have been excluded, as have all but the most important works on British history containing incidental coverage of Ireland. The typescript went to the printers in the summer of 1970, but, thanks to the co-operation of authors and publishers, it has been possible to insert a few items published since then.

The general arrangement of the bibliography is by subject, with the individual entries arranged alphabetically within each section or subsection. To facilitate cross-reference each entry has been allocated a running number, and this is printed in bold type wherever it occurs. Each item has been entered once only, with appropriate cross-references from other relevant sections. This has sometimes led to a scattering of related material, but it is hoped that the index will offset this disadvantage.

In accordance with editorial policy, the style of entry, abbreviations, etc. follow as far as possible the revised edition of T. W. Moody, 'Rules for contributors to *Irish Historical Studies*' in *I.H.S.*, suppl. I (1968), pp. 71-124. However, for the reasons outlined at the beginning of this introduction, and because of the special nature of the present work, a few minor deviations have been necessary, and in a few instances absolute consistency has been sacrificed in the interest of clarity. The aim throughout has been to give sufficient information to ensure correct identification and location, and to indicate the length and scope of each item, bearing in mind that the user may be dependent on photocopies and the inter-library loans service for articles in periodicals hard to come by outside a few major or specialised libraries. In the notes critical comment has been kept to a minimum, and attention has been concentrated on expounding the title where this is not self-explanatory, providing additional bibliographical information, and drawing attention to related or supplementary material and reviews. It should perhaps be pointed out that contents notes indicate an item's relevance to the present bibliography and do not necessarily give a balanced description of the work as a whole.

As far as possible a copy of each item has been checked at first hand, or in the form of an offprint or photocopy. However, it has been necessary to rely on information gleaned from published bibliographical sources for some variant editions and a few other items. Inevitably some omissions and other errors will have occurred, and space has been provided at the end of most sections for the insertion of addenda in individual copies. As this bibliography will be used as a quarry for subsequent bibliographical work connected with the *New history*, the author and the editors will be glad to hear of suggested amendments. These may be sent to the Secretary, *A new history of Ireland*, Royal Irish Academy, Dublin, 2.

ACKNOWLEDGEMENTS

Reference has been made in the introduction to the initial encouragement I received from my former teachers, Professors J. Otway-Ruthven and J. F. Lydon, and without their continuing enthusiasm this work would probably have foundered long before it reached the printers. They and Rev. Professor F. X. Martin, O.S.A., have given unstintingly of their time to advise on countless matters, read the entire work in typescript, drawn my attention to many items I would otherwise have missed, and saved me from many errors. Father Martin and Professor T. W. Moody have spent many hours considering and advising on typography, layout, and other aspects of production, and correcting proofs.

I am also greatly indebted to Mr Michael Dolley for his generous help with section XV. Dr R. E. Glasscock has kindly allowed me to use his as yet unpublished 'The making of the Irish landscape: a select bibliography of secondary works'. Mr F. H. A. Aalen, Mr Eamonn de hÓir, Dr C. A. Empey, Miss Marie-Thérèse Flanagan, Mr T. W. Graham, Mr K. W. Nicholls, and Rev. Peter O'Dwyer, O.Carm., have provided and checked several references and advised on a variety of matters. Dr Glasscock, Messrs G. K. Hall & Co., Cambridge University Press, Lutterworth Press, and the publications department of the Royal Irish Academy have supplied advance information which has enabled me to include a number of recent publications. Mr Richard Hawkins has checked many details which I was unable to check myself while the work was in the press. Mr Andrew Macmillan and Mr Conall Ó Catháin of Messrs Gillespie, Kidd & Coia, Glasgow, kindly acted as couriers for proofs during the British postal strike in 1971. A special word of thanks is due to my father for his assistance with the index, to my mother for her patient encouragement, and to Mr and Mrs P. C. Sugg for their hospitality on my visits to Dublin.

I have been deeply conscious throughout of my debt to the compilers of many published bibliographies, catalogues and reviews—too numerous to list here—and to the librarians and staffs of the institutions in which I did my research—the Catholic Central Library, Dublin, the National Library of Ireland, the National Library of Scotland, the Royal Irish Academy, the Royal Society of Antiquaries of Ireland, St Mary's Priory, Tallaght, Trinity College, Dublin—and to Mr R. O. MacKenna and my colleagues at Glasgow University Library.

I am most grateful to the board of editors of *A new history of Ireland* for financing the publication of this work, and to Mr W. D. Britton and the staff of Leinster Leader Ltd for the patience and skill they have displayed in printing it.

It remains for me to point out that expressing my gratitude to all those who have made this book possible does not exonerate me from sole responsibility for its errors and shortcomings.

P.W.A.

ABBREVIATIONS

Numbers in **bold** refer to entries in the present bibliography. For further details of most other periodicals see J. L. Kirby, *A guide to historical periodicals in the English language* (London: Historical Association, 1970. Helps for Students of History, no. 80).

These abbreviations follow, or are based on, those prescribed in *Rules for contributors to Irish Historical Studies* (Dublin, 1968).

A.H.R.	*The American Historical Review* (New York: American Historical Association, 1895-)
Abt.	Abteilung
Amer. Jn. Legal Hist.	*The American Journal of Legal History* (Philadelphia: Temple University School of Law, 1957-)
Anal. Bolland.	*Analecta Bollandiana* (Paris, Brussels: Société des Bollandistes, 1882-)
Anal. Hib.	*Analecta Hibernica*, see **54**
Arch. Jn.	*The Archaeological Journal* (London: Royal Archaeological Institute, 1845-)
Archives	*Archives: the journal of the British Records Association* (London, 1949-)
Aufl.	Auflage
B.M.	British Museum
Bd	Band
Belfast Natur. Hist. Soc. Proc.	*Proceedings and Reports of the Belfast Natural History and Philosophical Society*, see **105**
Brit. Acad. Proc.	*Proceedings of the British Academy* (London, 1904-)
C.I.E.	Córas Iompair Éireann
ch.	chapter
Cork Hist. Soc. Jn.	*Journal of the Cork Historical and Archaeological Society*, see **88**
Dept. Agric. Jn.	Department of Agriculture, Ireland, *Journal* (Dublin, 1900-). Name of issuing body varies.
Dublin Hist. Rec.	*Dublin Historical Record*, see **69**
E.H.R.	*The English Historical Review* (London, 1886-)
ed.; *ed.*	edited by; edition; editor(s)
éd.	édité par; édition
fasc.	fascicle
Féilscríbhinn Torna	Pender (S.), ed., *Essays and studies presented to Professor Tadhg Ua Donnchadha*, see **125**
Féil-sgríbhinn Eóin Mhic Néill	Ryan (J.), ed., *Essays and studies presented to Professor Eóin MacNeill*, see **126**
Galway Arch. Soc. Jn.	*Journal of the Galway Archaeological and Historical Society*, see **91**
H.C.	House of Commons
H.M.S.O.	Her (His) Majesty's Stationery Office
Hist. Studies	*Historical Studies*, see **73**
hrsg.	herausgegeben von
I.B.L.	*The Irish Book Lover* (Dublin, 1909-57)
I.C.H.S.	Irish Committee of Historical Sciences
I.C.H.S. Bull.	*Bulletin of the Irish Committee of Historical Sciences*, see **61**
I.E.R.	*The Irish Ecclesiastical Record*, see **77**
I.H.R. Bull.	*Bulletin of the Institute of Historical Research* (London, 1923-)
I.H.S.	*Irish Historical Studies*, see **80**
I.M.C.	Irish Manuscripts Commission

iml.	imleabhar
Ir. Ancestor	*The Irish Ancestor*, see **74**
Ir. Cath. Hist. Comm. Proc.	*Proceedings of the Irish Catholic Historical Committee*, see **106**
Ir. Geneal.	*The Irish Genealogist*, see **78**
Ir. Geography	*Irish Geography*, see **79**
Ir. Jurist	*The Irish Jurist*, see **81**
Ir. Lib. Bull.	*Irish Library Bulletin* (Dublin, 1940-51)
Ir. Rosary	*The Irish Rosary*, see **83**
Ir. Sword	*The Irish Sword*, see **84**
Ir. Theol. Quart.	*The Irish Theological Quarterly*, see **85**
Jn. Eccles. Hist.	*The Journal of Ecclesiastical History* (London, 1950-)
Jn. Relig. Hist.	*The Journal of Religious History* (Sydney, 1960-)
John Rylands Lib. Bull.	*Bulletin of the John Rylands Library* (Manchester, 1903-)
Kerry Arch. Soc. Jn.	*Journal of the Kerry Archaeological and Historical Society*, see **93**
Kildare Arch. Soc. Jn.	*Journal of the County Kildare Archaeological Society*, see **89**
Kilkenny Arch. Soc. Trans.	*Transactions of the Kilkenny Archaeological Society*, see **99**
Law Quart. Rev.	*The Law Quarterly Review* (London, 1885-)
Louth Arch. Soc. Jn.	*The Journal of the County Louth Archaeological Society*, see **90**
Med. studies presented to A. Gwynn	Watt (J. A.), Morrall (J. B.), Martin (F. X.), ed., *Medieval studies presented to Aubrey Gwynn*, see **129**
MS; MSS	manuscript; manuscripts
n.d.	no date
N.I. Legal Quart.	*The Northern Ireland Legal Quarterly* (Belfast, 1936-)
N. Munster Antiq. Jn.	*North Munster Antiquarian Journal*, see **102**
n.p.	no place
Nat. Mus. Ire.	National Museum of Ireland
no.; nos	number; numbers
O.S.	Ordnance Survey
P.	Press
p; pp	page; pages
P.R.N.I. Rep. D.K.	*Report of the Deputy Keeper of the Records, Northern Ireland*, see **48**
P.R.O.	Public Record Office, London
P.R.O.I.	Public Record Office of Ireland
pseud.	pseudonym
pt; pts	part; parts
R.E.	Radio Éireann
R. Hist. Soc. Trans.	*Transactions of the Royal Historical Society* (London, 1875-)
R.I.A.	Royal Irish Academy
R.I.A. Proc.	*Proceedings of the Royal Irish Academy*, see **107**
R.I.A. Trans.	*Transactions of the Royal Irish Academy*, see **117**
R.S.A.I.	Royal Society of Antiquaries of Ireland
R.S.A.I. Jn.	*Journal of the Royal Society of Antiquaries of Ireland*, see **99**
R.T.E.	Radio Telefís Éireann
repr.	reprint; reprinted

S.P.C.K.	Society for Promoting Christian Knowledge
Scot. Hist. Rev.	*The Scottish Historical Review* (Glasgow, etc., 1903-). Not published 1929-46
ser.	series
Soc. Archivists Jn.	*Journal of the Society of Archivists* (London, 1955-)
Speculum	*Speculum: a journal of mediaeval studies* (Cambridge, Mass.: Mediaeval Academy of America, 1926-)
Studia Celt.	*Studia Celtica* (Cardiff: Board of Celtic Studies, University of Wales, 1966-)
suppl.	supplement
T.	Teil
t.	tome
T.C.D.	Trinity College, Dublin
U.J.A.	*Ulster Journal of Archaeology*, see **119**
U.P.	University Press
Univ.	University
University Rev.	*University Review: official organ of the Graduates Association of the National University of Ireland* (Dublin, 1954-)
vol.; vols	volume; volumes
Waterford Arch. Soc. Jn.	*Journal of the Waterford and South East of Ireland Archaeological Society*, see **100**

1 BIBLIOGRAPHIES AND GUIDES

(a) GENERAL

See also **156, 173, 242.**

1 ANNUAL REPORT FROM THE AMERICAN COMMITTEE FOR IRISH STUDIES, 1st- , 1967/8- . In *I.H.S.*, xvi (1968-9)- .
Records the activities and publications of the committee, which was established in 1960. It has so far been concerned mainly with modern history.

2 ANNUAL REPORT OF THE IRISH COMMITTEE OF HISTORICAL SCIENCES, 1st- , 1938/9- . In *I.H.S.*, ii (1940-1)- .
Records the activities and plans of the Irish representative of the International Committee of Historical Sciences.

3 BRADY (John). The writings of Paul Walsh. In *I.H.S.*, iii (1942-3), 193-208.
A complete classified list of books, articles and reviews, including posthumous publications.

4 BROOKS (Eric St John). The sources for medieval Anglo-Irish history. In *Hist. Studies*, i (1958), 86-92.
A survey and guide to extant MS sources and transcripts, discussing the work of great collectors of the past and the present locations of collections.

5 DELANY (Vincent Thomas Hyginas). Ireland. In *Introduction bibliographique à l'histoire du droit et à l'ethnologie juridique: Bibliographical introduction to legal history and ethnology*, ed. John Gilissen (Bruxelles: Ministère de l'education nationale et de la culture, 1963- . Etudes d'Histoire et d'Ethnologie Juridiques), vol. C/6 (1963), pp 1-38.
A classified bibliography including much of interest to the historian.

6 EAGER (Alan Robert). A guide to Irish bibliographical material: being a bibliography of Irish bibliographies and some sources of information. Pp xiii, 392. London: Library Association, 1964.
A comprehensive list of bibliographical works on all aspects of Ireland, arranged approximately by the Dewey Decimal Classification, but without class numbers. Some standard works which are not bibliographies are included. Separate indexes of authors and subjects.

7 GLEESON (Dermot Florence). Sources for local history in the period 1200-1700. In *Cork Hist. Soc. Jn.*, xlvi (1941), 123-9.
A narrative survey of materials for Irish history. See also T. P. O'Neill, **32.**

8 GRIFFITH (Margaret Catherine). The Irish Record Commission, 1810-30. In *I.H.S.*, vii (1950-1), 17-38.

> An account of the commissioners' work and problems, with descriptive lists of reports, papers, transcripts, calendars, and repertories, including those never published, which are now an important source collection following the destruction of the originals in 1922.

9 GROSS (Charles). The sources and literature of English history from the earliest times to about 1485. Pp xx, 618. London: Longmans, Green, 1900; 2nd ed., revised and enlarged. Pp xxiii, 820. 1915.

> Includes many works relating to Ireland. These are scattered by subject, and are best located through the index.

10 GWYNN (Aubrey Osborn). Bibliographical note on medieval Anglo-Irish history. In *Hist. Studies*, i (1958), 93-9.

> A brief critical survey of the printed sources, with emphasis on those published since 1928.

11 GWYNN (Aubrey Osborn). Irlande: Ireland. In *Bibliographie de la Réforme, 1450-1648: ouvrages paru de 1940-1955* (Leiden: Brill, 1958-), fasc. 2 (1960), pp 49-61.

> An alphabetical list of books and articles, issued by Commission internationale d'histoire ecclésiastique comparée, International Committee of Historical Sciences.

12 HARDY (*Sir* Thomas Duffus). Descriptive catalogue of materials relating to the history of Great Britain and Ireland to the end of the reign of Henry VII. 3 vols in 4. London: Longman, Green, Longman & Roberts, 1862-71. (Rerum Britannicarum Medii Aevi Scriptores; or, Chronicles and Memorials of Great Britain and Ireland during the Middle Ages [*i.e.* Rolls Series, 26]); *repr.*, [Nendeln]: Kraus, 1964; New York: B. Franklin, 1964. (B. Franklin Bibliographical and Reference Series, no. 45).

> Not completed: ends at 1327. Printed and MS sources in a chronological sequence, with analytical notes and biographies of authors.

13 HAYES (Richard James), *ed.* The manuscript sources for the history of Irish civilization. 11 vols. Boston, Mass.: G. K. Hall, 1965.

> i-iv. Persons, including corporate bodies, except political and religious organisations.
> v-vi. Subjects, including political and religious organisations, and places outside Ireland.
> vii-viii. Places in Ireland, alphabetically within each county, with separate sequences for provinces, dioceses, and unidentified places.
> ix-x. Dates, by century, half-century, decade, year, and month—New Style throughout.

xi. Lists of manuscript catalogues of MSS, private collections, public and semi-public collections, Gaelic MSS in private and public collections; chronological lists of non-archival MSS prior to A.D. 1500, and of Gaelic MSS prior to 1900.

A descriptive index of MSS in 1,278 collections in 30 countries. It aims at completeness, but 87 MSS in T.C.D. have been inadvertently omitted; for these reference is made to *Catalogue of the manuscripts in the Library of Trinity College, Dublin,* compiled by T. K. Abbott (Dublin: Hodges, Figgis; London: Longmans, Green, 1900), and to *Catalogue of the Irish manuscripts in the Library of Trinity College, Dublin,* compiled by T. K. Abbott and E. J. Gwynn (Dublin: Hodges, Figgis, 1921).

14 HAYES (Richard James), *ed.* Sources for the history of Irish civilisation: articles in Irish periodicals. 9 vols. Boston, Mass.: G. K. Hall, 1970.

> i-v. Persons.
> vi-viii. Subjects.
> ix. Places in Ireland; dates.
> An index of *c.*280,000 articles and reviews in *c.*120 Irish periodicals, published *c.*1800-1969.

15 HOGAN (James). The Irish Manuscripts Commission: work in progress. Pp [6], 42. Cork: Cork U.P., 1954. (Irish Historical Series, no. 1)

> An account of the commission's work in its historical context, with a list of publications. Foreword by Denis Gwynn. See also **19**.

16 INSTITUTE OF HISTORICAL RESEARCH, *University of London.* Historical research for university degrees in the United Kingdom, 1931/32- . London: Longmans, Green, 1933- . (*I.H.R. Bull.,* Theses Supplements, nos 1-)

> Imprint varies: no. 13 (1952)- , London: Athlone P., 1953- .
> No. 19 (1957)- published in two parts: *Theses completed;* and *Theses in progress.*

17 IRISH CATHOLIC HISTORICAL COMMITTEE. A handlist of Irish diocesan histories. In *Ir. Cath. Hist. Comm. Proc.,* 1957, pp 31-7.

> A list of books (no articles), arranged under 20th-century Catholic diocese.

18 IRISH COMMITTEE OF HISTORICAL SCIENCES. BIBLIOGRAPHICAL SUB-COMMITTEE. Writings on Irish history, 1936- . *In I.H.S.,* i (1938-9)- .

> An annual list of books and articles in three sections: Serial publications containing material listed, Sources and guides, Secondary works; since 1967 the last two sections have been amalgamated. Lists of addenda are printed from time to time. The following categories of material are excluded: current reference works, parliamentary papers, writings on contemporary politics, newspaper articles, archaeological reports and literary and linguistic studies without reference to the historical context, and articles of little scholarly value.

19 IRISH MANUSCRIPTS COMMISSION. Catalogue of publications issued and in preparation, 1928-1966. Pp xiii, 79. Dublin: Stationery Office, 1966.

> A very detailed descriptive list of all the commission's works published, in preparation, and accepted for future publication. Includes full descriptions of the contents of *Analecta Hibernica*, **54**. Supersedes earlier editions. See also J. Hogan, **15**.

20 IRISH RECORD COMMISSION. Reports from the Commissioners appointed by His Majesty to execute the measures recommended in an address of the House of Commons, respecting the public records of Ireland. 1st-19th, 1810-1829. 5 vols. Dublin, London, 1815-30.

> 1st-5th, 1810-15. 1815.
> 6th-10th, 1816-20. 1820.
> 11th-15th, 1821-5. 1825.
> 16th & 17th, 1826-7, H.C. 1828 (50), xii, 455-76.
> 18th & 19th, 1828-9, H.C. 1830 (174), xvi, 129-53.
> Contents are summarised by M.C. Griffith in *I.H.S.*, vii (1950-1), 35-6.

21 JOHNSTON (Edith Mary). Irish history: a select bibliography. Pp 63. London: Historical Association, 1969. (Helps for Students of History, no. 73)

> An annotated introductory list.

22 KENNEY (James Francis). The sources for the early history of Ireland: an introduction and guide. Vol. i. Ecclesiastical. Pp xvi, 807. New York: Columbia U.P., 1929. (Records of Civilization: Sources and Studies, 11); 2nd ed. Pp xviii, 815. New York: Octagon Books; Shannon: Irish U.P., 1966.

> No more published. A detailed classified description of MS and printed sources, concerned primarily with the period before 1170, but including material indispensable to the student of the later middle ages. 2 maps. 2nd ed. is a corrected reprint with addenda and corrigenda by Ludwig Bieler (pp 791-8). A guide to sources, 1100-1534, is being prepared for I.M.C. under the editorship of J. F. Lydon.

23 LONGFIELD (Ada Katherine). List of published works [of H. G. Leask]. In *R.S.A.I. Jn.*, xcvi (1966), 3-6.

> A list of 81 monographs and articles. Author is Mrs Leask.

24 LYDON (James Francis Michael). Survey of the memoranda rolls of the Irish exchequer, 1294-1509. In *Anal. Hib.*, xxiii (1966), 49-134.

> A list of surviving extracts, aiming at comprehensiveness for Irish repositories, but probably omitting some undiscovered material in English collections. Introduction includes a descriptive list of subdivisions found in the rolls.

25 MARTIN (Francis Xavier). The historical writings of Reverend Professor Aubrey Gwynn, S.J. In *Med. studies presented to A. Gwynn* (1961), 502-9.

A chronological list of books, articles, and review articles.

26 MARTIN (Francis Xavier). The Thomas Davis lectures, 1953-67. In *I.H.S.*, xv (1966-7), 276-302.

A complete list, by date of broadcast, with bibliographical details of those published. Introductory essay.

27 MARTIN (Francis Xavier). The writings of Eoin MacNeill. In *I.H.S.*, vi (1948-9), 44-65.

A classified bibliography of published writings, including reviews, forewords, introductions and notes. Supersedes the 'Bibliography of the publications of Professor Mac Neill' in *Féil-sgríbhinn Eóin Mhic Néill* (1940), pp 581-3.

28 MOODY (Theodore William). The writings of Edmund Curtis. In *I.H.S.*, iii (1942-3), 393-400.

An annotated chronological list of historical writings, with an appendix of literary and journalistic writings, excluding reviews and occasional letters to the press. Short biographical appraisal (pp 393-5); for a fuller account see his 'Edmund Curtis, 1881-1943' in *Hermathena*, lxiii (May 1944), 69-78.

29 MULLINS (Edward Lindsay Carson). Texts and calendars: an analytical guide to serial publications. Pp xi, 674. London: Royal Historical Society, 1958. (Royal Historical Society Guides and Handbooks, no. 7)

Includes lists of P.R.O. calendars and other series containing volumes relating to Ireland.

30 O'HIGGINS (Paul). A bibliography of periodical literature relating to Irish law. Pp xvi, 401. Belfast: Northern Ireland Legal Quarterly, 1966.

A comprehensive classified list, with index.

31 O'HIGGINS (Paul). A select bibliography of Irish legal history. In *Amer. Jn. Legal Hist.*, iv (1960), 173-80; viii (1964), 261-3; xiii (1969), 233-40.

A short classified list of books and articles, with introductory notes to each section. See also **30**.

32 O'NEILL (Thomas Patrick). Sources of Irish local history. 1st series. Pp 38. Dublin: Library Association of Ireland, 1958.

Eight articles, reprinted from *An Leabharlann* (Dublin: Library Association of Ireland), xii (1954)-xv (1957), discussing annals, genealogies, lives of saints, *Leabhar na gCeart*, law tracts, ecclesiastical and legal records, maps and surveys, newspapers, pictures, tours, guide-books, gazetteers, directories, and British parliamentary papers. See also his 'Sources of local history, no. 9: Archives of local authorities' in *An Leabharlann*, xvi (1958), 31-6, the only part of the promised 2nd series to appear, and Dermot F. Gleeson, **7**.

33 RESEARCH ON IRISH HISTORY IN IRISH UNIVERSITIES, 1937/8- . In *I.H.S.*, i (1938-9)- .

Title varies: 'Research on Irish history in Irish, British and American universities', 1937/8-1939/41.

Annual lists of theses completed and in progress, arranged by university. Since 1941, lists for British and American universities have appeared occasionally, but reference should be made to **16**.

34 ROYAL HISTORICAL SOCIETY. Writings on British history, 1901-1933. 5 vols in 7. London: Cape, 1968-70.

Vol. ii. *The middle ages, 450-1485*. Pp 347. 1968.

Includes a list of writings on Ireland having a direct bearing on English history (pp 262-4), and some other relevant works are listed elsewhere by subject. The work is complementary to *A guide to the historical and archaeological publications of societies in England and Wales, 1901-1933*, compiled for the Institute of Historical Research by E. L. C. Mullins (London: Athlone P., 1968), and is supplemented by the Royal Historical Society's annual *Writings on British history, 1934-1939*, compiled by A. T. Milne (6 vols, London: Cape, 1937-53) and cumulative *Writings on British history, 1940-45*, compiled by A. T. Milne (2 vols, London: Cape, 1960).

35 ROYAL IRISH ACADEMY. Index to the serial publications of the Royal Irish Academy (Transactions, Proceedings, Cunningham memoirs, Todd lecture series, and Irish manuscript series) from 1786 to 1906 inclusive. Pp x, 116. Dublin: Hodges, Figgis; London: Williams & Norgate, 1912.—Index to the serial publications of the Royal Irish Academy (Proceedings, Cunningham memoirs, Todd lecture series) from 1907 to 1932. Pp 27. Dublin: Hodges, Figgis; London: Williams & Norgate, 1934.—Index to the serial publications of the Royal Irish Academy (Proceedings, Cunningham memoirs, Todd lecture series) from 1932 to 1953. Pp [4], 40. Dublin: Hodges, Figgis, 1959.

Each lists authors, titles, and subjects in a single sequence. Preface in *Index . . . 1786-1906* contains a bibliographical history of each series.

36 THIRTY YEARS' WORK IN IRISH HISTORY. In *I.H.S.*, xv (1966-7), 359-90; xvi (1968-9), 1-32; xvii (1970-1), 1-31, 151-84.

A series of articles on progress in research, noting the more important publications. Includes A. J. Otway-Ruthven, 'Medieval Ireland, 1169-1485' in *I.H.S.*, xv (1966-7), 359-65. See also T. W. Moody, 'A new history of Ireland' in *I.H.S.*, xvi (1968-9), 241-57.

(b) GUIDES TO REPOSITORIES

(i) Public Record Office of Ireland

37 DARWIN (Kenneth). The Irish record situation. In *Soc. Archivists Jn.*, ii (1960-4), 361-6.

38 GRIFFITH (Margaret Catherine). A short guide to the Public Record Office of Ireland. In *I.H.S.*, viii (1952-3), 45-58; *repr.* Pp 14. Dublin: Stationery Office, 1952; 2nd ed. Pp 16. 1964.
> A summary account of the contents of the office, subdivided as incremental records (testamentary, courts, State Paper Office), departmental, parochial, and non-official. Notes the existence of detailed lists, indexes, etc. Omits records remaining in the State Paper Office.

39 MURRAY (Robert Henry). A short guide to the principal classes of documents preserved in the Public Record Office, Dublin. Pp iii, 64. London: S.P.C.K., 1919. (Helps for Students of History, no. 7)
> A short narrative survey of what then existed, with an appendix on MSS in Marsh's Library, Dublin, Armagh Public Library, N.L.I., and R.I.A. See also H. Wood, **42**.

40 REPORT OF THE DEPUTY KEEPER OF THE PUBLIC RECORDS IN IRELAND. 1st- . Dublin: H.M.S.O., 1869- .
> Title varies: *Report of the Deputy Keeper of the Public Records and Keeper of the State Papers in Ireland*, 25th- , 1893- .
> Imprint varies: 53rd (1921)- , Dublin, Stationery Office, 1926- .
> Indexes: 1st-5th, in *5* (1873), 88-91; 6th-10th, in *10* (1878), 39-56; 11th-15th, in *15* (1883), 185-91; 16th-20th, in *20* (1888), 123-38; 21st-25th, in *25* (1893), 41-52; 26th-30th, in *30* (1898), 62-70; 31st-40th, in *40* (1908), 33-41.
> Published as command papers, 1869-1920. Appendices include catalogues, calendars and indexes of many important records destroyed in 1922.

41 WOOD (Herbert). British and allied archives during the war: Ireland. In *R. Hist. Soc. Trans.*, 4th ser., ii (1919), 26-32.
> A brief survey of Irish public records in 1918 and their history during the First World War.

42 WOOD (Herbert). A guide to the records deposited in the Public Record Office of Ireland, Pp xvi, 334. Dublin: H.M.S.O., 1919.
> Now invaluable for its description of documents destroyed in 1922. The records are listed and described under the body from which they emanate. Historical introduction, and index.

43 WOOD (Herbert). The public records of Ireland before and after 1922. In *R. Hist. Soc. Trans.*, 4th ser., xiii (1930), 17-49.

A review of their history and destruction, with an account of what has been saved, and the extent to which the loss of the remainder is mitigated by transcripts, calendars, etc.

44 WOOD (Herbert). The tragedy of the Irish public records. In *Ir. Geneal.*, i (1937-42), 67-71.

Recounts their history and destruction.

(ii) Public Record Office of Northern Ireland

45 CHART (David Alfred). The Public Record Office of Northern Ireland, 1924-36. In *I.H.S.*, i (1938-9), 42-57.

Traces the origins and history of the office and the development of its collections of material concerning Ulster. Includes an index to the principal collections and chief historical topics treated in *P.R.N.I. Rep. D.K. 1924-36*, see **48**.

46 DARWIN (Kenneth). The Public Record Office of Northern Ireland. In *Archives*, vi (1963-4), 108-16.

A description of its history, scope, contents and activities. The office contains little medieval material.

47 DARWIN (Kenneth). The Public Record Office of Northern Ireland. In *Ir. Ancestor*, i (1969), 11-16.

A short account of its work and facilities.

48 PUBLIC RECORD OFFICE OF NORTHERN IRELAND. Report of the Deputy Keeper of the Records for the year 1924- . Belfast: H.M.S.O., 1925- .

Published as Northern Ireland command papers. Annual, 1924-37; thereafter frequency varies, each report usually covering a number of years. They include detailed lists of deposits and indexes as appendices, and together form the only comprehensive guide to the contents of the office. For an index, 1924-36, see D. A. Chart, **45**.

(iii) Public Record Office, London

49 GUIDE TO THE CONTENTS OF THE PUBLIC RECORD OFFICE. London: H.M.S.O., 1963- . *In progress.*

Vol. i. *Legal records, etc.* Pp vi, 249. 1963.
Vol. ii. *State papers and departmental records.* Pp vii, 410. 1963.
Vol. iii. *Documents transferred, 1960-1966.* Pp vii, 191. 1968.

Vol. iii also includes 'Corrigenda and addenda' to vols i-ii. The office contains a great deal of material relating to Ireland; most of the medieval records are described in vol. i. The work as a whole supersedes earlier editions: S. R. Scargill-Bird, *A guide to the principal classes of documents preserved in the Public Record Office* (London: H.M.S.O., 1891; 3rd ed., 1908); M. S. Giuseppi, *A guide to the manuscripts preserved in the Public Record Office* (2 vols, London: H.M.S.O., 1923-4).

(iv) British Museum

50 CATALOGUE OF IRISH MANUSCRIPTS IN THE BRITISH MUSEUM. 3 vols.
London: Trustees of the British Museum, 1926-53.
> Vol. i, by Standish Hayes O'Grady; vol. ii, by Robin Flower; vol. iii,
> by R. Flower, revised by Myles Dillon.
> A classified descriptive list (vols i-ii), with introduction, indexes, and
> facsimiles (vol. iii).

(v) Vatican Archives

51 CORISH (Patrick Joseph). Irish history and the papal archives. In
Ir. Theol. Quart., xxi (1954), 375-81.
> A brief account of the contents of the Vatican Archives and their
> significance for Irish historians.

52 FINK (Karl August). Das Vatikanische Archiv: Einführung in die
Bestände und ihre Erforschung. 2. vermehrte Aufl. Pp xii, 185.
Rom: W. Regenburg, 1951.
> The best comprehensive guide to a collection of great importance for
> the study of medieval Ireland. Supersedes earlier general guides. For a
> more detailed account of the medieval records see Leonard Boyle,
> *A survey of the Vatican Archives and of its medieval holdings* (Toronto:
> Pontifical Academy of Medieval Studies), to be published in 1971. See
> also Christopher R. Cheney, *The study of the medieval papal chancery*
> (Glasgow: Jackson, 1966. Glasgow University Publications, The Edwards
> Lectures, 2)

53 MACFARLANE (Leslie). The Vatican Archives; with special reference
to sources for British medieval history. In *Archives*, iv (1959-60),
29-44, 84-101.
> Also published separately as an offprint. An invaluable short introduction,
> including a description of the contents and present-day organisation.

II SERIALS

See also **40, 48, 150, 156, 655.**

54 ANALECTA HIBERNICA. Dublin: Stationery Office, 1930-69; Shannon: Irish U.P., 1970- . (I.M.C.)
> Irregular serial containing material not suitable for publication in I.M.C. monograph series, **82,** including reports on the work of I.M.C. Nos v (1934), ix (1940), xiii (1944), xix (1957) are indexes to those numbers not separately indexed. For a detailed description of the contents of each number, see **19.**

55 ARCHIVIUM HIBERNICUM; OR, IRISH HISTORICAL RECORDS. i-vii. Maynooth: Record Society, 1912-21; New ser., viii- . Maynooth: Catholic Record Society of Ireland, 1941- .
> Frequency varies. Includes guides to source collections.

56 ASSISI: IRISH FRANCISCAN MONTHLY. 34 vols. Dublin: Irish Province of the Order of Friars Minor, 1929-65.
> Continued as *Brief of St Anthony of Padua,* **60.**

57 BÉALOIDEAS: THE JOURNAL OF THE FOLKLORE OF IRELAND SOCIETY. Dublin: The Society, 1927- .
> Society also called An Cumann le Béaloideas Éireann. Annual since vol. x (1940), but usually published late with two dates on the title-page.

58 BREIFNE: JOURNAL OF CUMANN SEANCHAIS BHREIFNE (BREIFNE HISTORICAL SOCIETY). Cavan: The Society, 1958- .
> Annual nos, forming vol. every 4 years.

59 BREIFNY ANTIQUARIAN SOCIETY. Journal. 3 vols. Cavan: The Society, 1920-33.
> No indexes.

60 BRIEF OF ST ANTHONY OF PADUA. Dublin: Irish Province of the Order of Friars Minor, 1966- .
> Formerly *Assisi,* **56.**

61 BULLETIN OF THE IRISH COMMITTEE OF HISTORICAL SCIENCES. Dublin: I.C.H.S., 1939- .
> Nos 1-59 (1939-48); New ser., i- , no. 60- (1952-).
> *Titles of papers summarized in nos 1-33 (Dec. 1939-May 1944), with the names of the contributors arranged alphabetically.* 1944; *Table of contents and index to contributors, [nos 34-58, Nov. 1944 to May 1948].* n.d.; *Index, nos 60-88, 1952-1959.* n.d.
> Mainly typescript summaries of papers read to I.C.H.S., many of which have subsequently appeared *in extenso* in *I.H.S.* and elsewhere. Frequency varies.

62 CARLOVIANA: THE JOURNAL OF THE OLD CARLOW SOCIETY. [Carlow: The Society], 1947- .
    Vol. i. 3 pts. 1947-9; New ser., i- . 1952- .
    Annual parts, each separately paginated.

63 CELTIC SOCIETY. [Publications.] 6 vols. Dublin: The Society, 1847-53.
    Amalgamated with Irish Archaeological Society to form Irish Archaeological and Celtic Society, 75.

64 CLOGHER RECORD. Monaghan: Cumann Seanchais Chlochair (The Historical Society of the Diocese of Clogher), 1953- .
    Annual parts; 3 parts per vol. Each part of vol. i separately paginated.

65 CLONMEL HISTORICAL AND ARCHAEOLOGICAL SOCIETY. Journal of the proceedings: meetings, papers, discussions, and exhibits. Vol. i, nos 1-4. Clonmel: The Society, 1952-6.
    Reprinted from *The Nationalist*.

66 COLLECTANEA HIBERNICA: SOURCES FOR IRISH HISTORY. Shannon: Irish U.P., 1958- .
    Imprint varies: i-viii, Dublin: Clonmore & Reynolds; London: Burns, Oates & Washbourne, 1958-65; ix-x, Dublin: Assisi P., 1966-7.
    Annual. Directed by the Franciscan Fathers at the Franciscan House of Celtic Studies and Historical Research, Killiney, Co. Dublin. Includes guides to sources.

67 DONEGAL ANNUAL: JOURNAL OF THE COUNTY DONEGAL HISTORICAL SOCIETY. [n.p.]: The Society, 1947- .
    Title varies: i (1947-50): *Journal of the County Donegal Historical Society: Iris Cumann Seanchais Dún na nGall*.

68 DOWN AND CONNOR HISTORICAL SOCIETY'S JOURNAL. 10 vols. Belfast: The Historical Society of the Clergy and Laity of Down and Connor, 1928-39.
    Title varies: vol. i (1928): *Down and Connor Historical Society's Magazine*.

69 DUBLIN HISTORICAL RECORD. Dublin: Old Dublin Society, 1938- .
    Quarterly.

70 ÉRIU: THE JOURNAL OF THE SCHOOL OF IRISH LEARNING. 9 vols. Dublin: The School, 1904-23; *continued as* ÉRIU. x- . Dublin: R.I.A., 1926- .
    Not published 1924-5.

71 GALVIA: IRISLEABHAR CHUMANN SEANDÁLUÍOCHTA IS STAIRE NA GAILLIMHE. Galway: Galway Archaeological and Historical Society, 1954- .
    Annual. All articles in Irish. See also 91.

72 HERMATHENA: A DUBLIN UNIVERSITY REVIEW. Dublin: Hodges, Figgis; London: Academic P., 1873- .

Title varies: nos 1-96 (1873-1962): *Hermathena: a series of papers on literature, science and philosophy by members of Trinity College, Dublin.* Imprint varies: vols i-iii (nos 1-6), Dublin: Edward Ponsonby; London: Longmans, Green, 1874-9; vols iv-xx (nos 7-45), nos 46-78, Dublin: Hodges, Figgis; London: Longmans, Green, 1880-1951; nos 79-97, Dublin: Hodges, Figgis, 1952-63.

Index of contributors to Hermathena, 1873-1943, by J. G. Smyly. Pp 29. Dublin: Hodges, Figgis; London: Longmans, Green, [1944]; 'Index to Hermathena, 1944-64', [by E. J. J. Furlong] in *Hermathena*, no. 101 (Autumn 1965), pp 48-59.

Half-yearly; each part separately paginated. Two supplemental vols, 1927.

73 HISTORICAL STUDIES: PAPERS READ BEFORE THE IRISH CONFERENCE OF HISTORIANS. London: Routledge & Kegan Paul, 1958- .

i. 2nd, [*Dublin, 1955*]; ed. T. Desmond Williams. 1958.
ii. 3rd, [*Belfast, 1957*]; ed. Michael Roberts. 1959.
iii. 4th, [*Cork, 1959*]; ed. James Hogan. 1961.
iv. 5th, [*Galway, 1961*]; ed. G. A. Hayes-McCoy. 1963.
v. 6th, [*Londonderry, 1963*]; ed. J. L. McCracken. 1965.
vi. [*7th*], *Dublin, 1965*; ed. T. W. Moody. 1968.
vii. [*8th, Belfast, 1967*]; ed. J. C. Beckett. 1969.
Imprint varies: i-v, London: Bowes & Bowes. Vols ii and v have error in subtitle: 'Conference of Irish Historians'—see T. W. Moody in *Hist. Studies*, vi (1965), pp vii-viii.

74 THE IRISH ANCESTOR. Dublin: Irish Ancestor, 1969- .
Annual.

75 IRISH ARCHAEOLOGICAL AND CELTIC SOCIETY. [Publications.] 10 vols in 13. Dublin: The Society, 1855-80.
Imprint varies: vii, Calcutta, 1868.
See also **63**, **76**.

76 IRISH ARCHAEOLOGICAL SOCIETY. [Publications.] 19 vols in 15. Dublin: The Society, 1841-51.
Amalgamated with Celtic Society to form Irish Archaeological and Celtic Society, **75**.

77 THE IRISH ECCLESIASTICAL RECORD: A MONTHLY JOURNAL. 171 vols. Dublin: Browne & Nolan, 1864-1968.
i (1864-5)-iv (1867-8); [New ser.], v (1868-9)-xii (1875-6); 3rd ser., i (1880)-xvii (1896); 4th ser., i (1897)-xxxii (1912); 5th ser., i (1913)-cx (1968).
Imprint varies: vols i-iv, Dublin: John F. Fowler, 1864-8; new ser., v-xii, Dublin: William B. Kelly; London: Burns & Oates; New York: P. M. Haverty, 1868-76.

'Index, 1864-1917: documents' in *I.E.R.*, 5th ser., xcii (1959), suppl., pp 1*-44*; 'Subject and author index, 1864-1917: articles, correspondence, notes and queries (theology, canon law, liturgy)' in *I.E.R.*, 5th ser., xcviii (1962), suppl., pp 1-60; 'Index, 1864-1917: reviews' in *I.E.R.*, 5th ser., xcviii (1962), suppl., pp 61-70; repr. as *Index to the Irish Ecclesiastical Record, 1864-1917: documents, articles, correspondence and reviews*. Pp 44*, 70. Dublin: Browne & Nolan, 1963; 'Subject and author index, 1918-1963' in *I.E.R.*, 5th ser., cii (1964), 297-344; also published separately, or bound with *Index, 1864-1917*, 1964. All indexes compiled by Patrick J. Hamell.

Periodical not published 1877-9. 2 vols per annum, 1897-1968, except 5th ser., lxix (1947), lxx (1948). Edited from St Patrick's College, Maynooth. See 'The Irish Ecclesiastical Record, 1864-1964' in *I.E.R.*, 5th ser., cii (1964), 263-78, which contains a brief history by Thomas Wall, with lists of editors, correspondents and authors, and reprints a key to contributors' initials originally published in 3rd ser., ii (1881). See also Denis Gwynn, 'The scope of the "Record" ' in *I.E.R.*, 5th ser., cii (1964), 224-35.

78 THE IRISH GENEALOGIST: OFFICIAL ORGAN OF THE IRISH GENEALOGICAL RESEARCH SOCIETY. London: The Society, 1937- .
Annual.

79 IRISH GEOGRAPHY: BULLETIN OF THE GEOGRAPHICAL SOCIETY OF IRELAND. Dublin: The Society, 1944- .
Title varies: vol. i, nos 1-3 (1944-6): *Bulletin of the Geographical Society of Ireland*.
Annual.

80 IRISH HISTORICAL STUDIES: THE JOINT JOURNAL OF THE IRISH HISTORICAL SOCIETY AND THE ULSTER SOCIETY FOR IRISH HISTORICAL STUDIES. Dublin: Dublin U.P., 1938- .
Imprint varies: vols i-xv, Dublin: Hodges, Figgis, 1938-67.
'Index to Irish Historical Studies, vols i-xv', by Esther Semple in *I.H.S.*, suppl. i (1968), pp 8-70.
Half-yearly. See also **1, 2, 18**.

81 THE IRISH JURIST. Dublin: The Jurist Publishing Co., University College, 1935- .
Vols. i-xxxi (1935-65); New ser., i- (1966-).
Half-yearly. Cf. earlier periodical with this title, Dublin, 1849-67.

82 IRISH MANUSCRIPTS COMMISSION. [Publications.] Shannon: Irish U.P., 1931- .
Imprint varies: Dublin: Stationery Office, 1931-69.
For catalogue, see **19**. See also **54**.

83 THE IRISH ROSARY. Dublin: Dominican Publications, St Saviour's, 1897- .
Issued every 2 months.

84 THE IRISH SWORD: THE JOURNAL OF THE MILITARY HISTORY SOCIETY OF IRELAND. Dublin: The Society, 1949- .
Half-yearly.

85 THE IRISH THEOLOGICAL QUARTERLY. Maynooth: St Patrick's College, 1906- .
New ser., 1951- , but volumes numbered consecutively with original series. Not published, 1923-50.

86 THE JOURNAL OF THE ARDAGH AND CLONMACNOISE ANTIQUARIAN SOCIETY. 2 vols in 12. Dublin: James Duffy, 1926-51.
Each part independently paginated.

87 JOURNAL OF THE BUTLER SOCIETY. Kilkenny: The Society, 1968- .
Annual.

88 JOURNAL OF THE CORK HISTORICAL AND ARCHAEOLOGICAL SOCIETY. Cork: The Society, 1892- .
i-iii, 1892-4; 2nd ser., i- , 1895- .
Index, 1892-1940. Pp [5], 104. 1943; *Index, 1941-1960.* Pp iv, 54. 1964. Both compiled by Denis J. O'Donoghue.
Annual. Not published for 1923.

89 JOURNAL OF THE COUNTY KILDARE ARCHAEOLOGICAL SOCIETY. [n.p.]: The Society, 1891- .
Frequency varies.

90 THE JOURNAL OF THE COUNTY LOUTH ARCHAEOLOGICAL SOCIETY. Dundalk: Dundalgan P., for the Society, 1904- .
Cover title: *County Louth Archaeological Journal.*
Annual. 4 pts of vol. i separately paginated.
[Index to vols i-xiii, 1904-57] in *Louth Arch. Soc. Jn.*, xiv (1957-60), 232-78.

91 JOURNAL OF THE GALWAY ARCHAEOLOGICAL AND HISTORICAL SOCIETY. Galway: The Society, 1900- .
Biannual.
Index to volumes i to vii, inclusive, [1900-12]; compiled by Myrrha Bradshaw and Jacqueline Dowie. Pp xxiii, 166. Dublin: John Falconer, 1913.

92 THE JOURNAL OF THE IRISH MEMORIALS ASSOCIATION. 13 vols.
Dublin: The Association, 1888-1937.
Title varies: vol. i (1888-91): *Fund for the Preservation of the Memorials of the Dead, Ireland. Report;* vols ii-iii (1892-7): *Association for the Preservation of the Memorials of the Dead, Ireland. Journal;* vols iv-x (1900-20): *Journal of the Association for the Preservation of the Memorials of the Dead in Ireland.*
An index of the churchyards and buildings from which inscriptions on tombs and mural slabs have appeared in the Journal of the Association for the Preservation of the Memorials of the Dead in Ireland, from 1888 to 1908, inclusive. Pp [41]. 1909; *Consolidated index of surnames and place-names to volumes i to vii (1888-1909).* Pp 238. 1914.

93 JOURNAL OF THE KERRY ARCHAEOLOGICAL AND HISTORICAL SOCIETY.
[n.p.]: Cumann Seandálaíochta is Staire Chiarraí, 1968- .
Annual.

94 JOURNAL OF THE LIMERICK FIELD CLUB. 3 vols. Limerick: The
Club, 1897-1908.
Continued by *Journal of the North Munster Archaeological Society*, **95**.
For index see **95**.

95 JOURNAL OF THE NORTH MUNSTER ARCHAEOLOGICAL SOCIETY.
4 vols. Limerick: The Society, 1909-19.
Continues *Journal of the Limerick Field Club*, **94**. Revived as *North Munster Antiquarian Journal*, **102.**
Index to Journal, 1897-1919, by Dermot Foley. Pp 26. [Limerick: Thomond Archaeological Society, 1958.]

96 JOURNAL OF THE OLD ATHLONE SOCIETY. [Athlone: The Society],
1969- .
Annual.

97 JOURNAL OF THE OLD LIMERICK SOCIETY (CUMANN SEANDACHTA
LUIMNIGHE). Limerick: The Society, 1946.
Only one issue published.

98 JOURNAL OF THE OLD WEXFORD SOCIETY. [Wexford: The Society],
1968- .
Annual.

99 THE JOURNAL OF THE ROYAL SOCIETY OF ANTIQUARIES OF IRELAND.
Dublin: The Society, 1849- .
Title varies: vols i-ii (1849-53): *Transactions of the Kilkenny Archaeological Society;* vol. iii (1854-5): *Proceedings and Transactions of the Kilkenny and South-East Ireland Archaeological Society;* New ser., i-vi [Consecutive ser., iv-ix] (1856-67): *Journal of the Kilkenny and South-East Ireland Archaeological Society;* 3rd ser., i [Consecutive ser., x]

(1868-9): *Journal of the Historical and Archaeological Association of Ireland;* 4th ser., i-ix [Consecutive ser., xi-xix] (1870-89): *Journal of the Royal Historical and Archaeological Association of Ireland;* 5th ser., i [Consecutive ser., xxi] (1890-1): *Journal of Proceedings of the Royal Society of Antiquaries of Ireland;* 5th ser., ii-xx [Consecutive ser., xxii-xl], 1892-1910; 6th ser., i-xx, Consecutive ser., xli-lx, 1911-30; 7th ser., i-xiv, Consecutive ser., lxi-lxxiv, 1931-44; thereafter numbered only as Consecutive ser., lxxv-   , 1945-   .

Frequency varies. References usually refer to Consecutive series, unless otherwise specified.

Index, i-xix, 1849-1889 as 4th ser., x [Consecutive ser., xx]. Pp 268. 1902. (Extra vol. for 1898-1901); *Index, xxi-xl, 1891-1910.* Pp 265. 1915. (Extra vol.); *Index, xli-lx, 1911-1930.* Pp 226. 1933. (Extra vol.)

Vol. lxxix (1949): *Centenary volume.*

Vol. xcv (1965): *Papers in honour of Liam Price.*

See also **111**.

100 JOURNAL OF THE WATERFORD & SOUTH-EAST OF IRELAND ARCHAEOLOGICAL SOCIETY. 19 vols. Waterford: The Society, 1894-1920.

Vol. xix not completed: no. 1, January 1920 only. Not published 1916-19.

101 MEDIEVAL IRISH HISTORY SERIES. Dublin: Dublin Historical Association, 1964-   .

Imprint varies: No. 1, Dundalk: Dundalgan P., for the Dublin Historical Association.

A series of pamphlets, published at irregular intervals.

102 NORTH MUNSTER ANTIQUARIAN JOURNAL. Limerick: The Thomond Archaeological Society, 1936-   .

Issuing body, Vols i-iii (1936-41): The Thomond Archaeological Society and Field Club.

Frequency varies. 4 pts of vol. vii (1954-7) independently paginated.

Revival of lapsed *Journal of the North Munster Archaeological Society,* **95**.

103 OLD KILKENNY REVIEW: THE JOURNAL OF THE KILKENNY ARCHAEOLOGICAL SOCIETY. Kilkenny: The Society, 1948-   .

Annual.

'Catalogue of articles in . . . nos 1-12, [1948-60]' in no. 13 (1961), 35-9.

104 THE PAST: ORGAN OF THE UI CEINNSEALAIGH HISTORICAL SOCIETY. Enniscorthy: The Society, 1920-   .

Frequency varies.

105 PROCEEDINGS AND REPORTS OF THE BELFAST NATURAL HISTORY AND PHILOSOPHICAL SOCIETY. 74 vols. Belfast: The Society, 1873-1955.

Title varies: 1871/72-1881/82: *Proceedings. . .* ; 1882/83-1919/20: *Report and Proceedings. . . .*

Ser. 2, i-xx (1935/36-1954/55).

Before 1871/72, 'Proceedings' were published in *The Natural History Review* (Dublin) and separately as untitled leaflets.

Contents mainly scientific, but include several historical papers, especially after the establishment of the archaeological section in 1917.

106 PROCEEDINGS OF THE IRISH CATHOLIC HISTORICAL COMMITTEE.
Dublin: The Committee, 1955- .
Irregular. Some papers also published in *I.E.R.*, **77**.

107 PROCEEDINGS OF THE ROYAL IRISH ACADEMY. Dublin: The Academy,
1836- .
Imprint varies: Dublin: Hodges, Figgis, 1904-64.
Published in three subject sections since 1902 (Section C. Archaeology,
linguistic and literature), but volumes numbered consecutively from 1836.
Each item issued as a separate fascicle, paginated continuously for each
section of the volume, which thus has three sequences of pages.
For indexes, see **35**. See also **110, 117**.

108 REPORTORIUM NOVUM: DUBLIN DIOCESAN HISTORICAL RECORD.
Dublin: Browne & Nolan, 1955- .
Imprint varies: Vol. i, Dublin: C. J. Fallon, 1955-6.
Annual.

109 RÍOCHT NA MIDHE: RECORDS OF MEATH ARCHAEOLOGICAL AND
HISTORICAL SOCIETY. [Trim]: The Society, 1955- .
Annual. Each part of vols i and ii separately paginated.

110 ROYAL IRISH ACADEMY. Minutes of proceedings. Session 1930/31- .
Dublin: The Academy, 1932- .
Annual.

111 ROYAL SOCIETY OF ANTIQUARIES OF IRELAND. Extra volumes.
Dublin: The Society, 1870- .
Issuing body, 1870-89: Royal Historical and Archaeological Association
of Ireland.
Monograph series, published at irregular intervals. See also **99**.

112 SEANCHAS ARDMHACHA: JOURNAL OF THE ARMAGH DIOCESAN
HISTORICAL SOCIETY. Armagh: The Society, 1954- .
Annual. Each part of vol. i (1954-5) independently paginated.

113 STUDIA HIBERNICA. Baile Átha Cliath: Coláiste Phádraig, 1961- .
Annual.

114 STUDIES: AN IRISH QUARTERLY REVIEW OF LETTERS, PHILOSOPHY
AND SCIENCE. Dublin: Talbot P., 1912- .
General index of volumes 1-50, 1912-1961; [compiled by Aloysius
O'Rahilly]. Pp 319. Ros Cré (Roscrea): An Fáisceán Liath, 1966.

115 TEATHBHA: JOURNAL OF THE LONGFORD HISTORICAL SOCIETY.
Longford: The Society, 1969- .
Society also called Cumann Seanchais Longfoirt.

116 TRANSACTIONS OF THE OSSORY ARCHAEOLOGICAL SOCIETY. 3 vols. Kilkenny: The Society, 1879-86.
Vol. iii not completed: pts 1 and 2 only published.

117 TRANSACTIONS OF THE ROYAL IRISH ACADEMY. 33 vols. Dublin: The Academy, 1787-1907.
Vol. xxxii (1902-4) published in 3 independently paginated sections (Section C: Archaeology, linguistic and literature). For index see **35**. See also **107**.

118 ULSTER FOLKLIFE. Belfast: Committee on Ulster Folklife and Traditions, 1955- .
Annual.

119 ULSTER JOURNAL OF ARCHAEOLOGY. 9 vols. Belfast: Archer; Dublin: Hodges & Smith; London: J. Russell Smith, 1853-62; New ser. 17 vols. Belfast: Marcus Ward, 1895-8; McCaw, Stevenson & Orr, 1899-1911; 3rd ser. Belfast: Ulster Archaeological Society, 1938- .
Annual. New ser., xvii (1911) not completed.
Index and corrigenda, 3rd ser., vol. 1 (1938) to vol. 6 (1943). Pp 36. 1944; *Index, vol. vii (1944) to vol. xii (1949),* prepared by Mrs I. R. Crozier. Pp 24. [1954]; *Index, volumes 13 (1950)-30 (1967),* compiled by L. N. W. Flanagan in *U.J.A.*, 3rd ser., xxx (1967), 101-28.
2 *Extra volumes* issued with New ser. For supplement to 3rd ser., see **364**.

III ESSAYS, FESTSCHRIFTEN, ETC.

See also **99, 329, 584.**

120 BELFAST IN ITS REGIONAL SETTING: A SCIENTIFIC SURVEY. Prepared for the meeting held in Belfast, 3rd to 10th September, 1952. Pp 211. Belfast: British Association for the Advancement of Science, 1952.

121 CLARKE (Maude Violet). Fourteenth century studies. Edited by L. S. Sutherland and May McKisack. Pp xxi, 317. Oxford: Clarendon P., 1937; *repr.* 1969.

122 DOOLIN (William) *and* FITZGERALD (Oliver), *ed.* What's past is prologue: a retrospect of Irish medicine. Presented by the Monument Press on the occasion of the joint meeting of the British and Irish Medical Associations in Dublin, July 1952. Pp 97. [Dublin: Monument P., 1952.]

123 JENKINS (Geraint), *ed.* Studies in folk life: essays in honour of Iorwerth C. Peate. Pp xvii, 344. London: Routledge & Kegan Paul, 1969.

124 MEENAN (James) *and* WEBB (David Allardyce), *ed.* A view of Ireland: twelve essays on different aspects of Irish life and the Irish countryside. Pp xv, 254. Dublin: British Association for the Advancement of Science, 1957.

125 PENDER (Séamus), *ed.* Essays and studies presented to Professor Tadhg Ua Donnchadha (Torna), on the occasion of his seventieth birthday, September 4th, 1944. Pp 258. Cork: Cork U.P., 1947.
Added title-page: *Féilscríbhinn Torna .i. Tráchtaisí léanta in onóir don Ollamh Tadhg Ua Donnchadha, D.Litt., in am a dheichiú bliana agus trí fichid, an ceathrú lá de mhí Mheán Fhómhair, 1944 . . . .*

126 RYAN (John), *ed.* Essays and studies presented to Professor Eoin MacNeill, D.Litt., on the occasion of his seventieth birthday, May 15th, 1938. Pp xv, 593. Dublin: Three Candles, 1940.
Added title-page: *Féil-sgríbhinn Eóin Mhic Néill .i. Tráchtair léigheanta i n-onóir do'nollamhain Eóin Mac Néill, D.Litt., do sgríobh cáirde d'á cháirdibh i n-am a bheichmhadh bliadhna agus trí fichid, an cúigmhadh lá déag de mhí na Bealtaine, 1938.*

127 RYNNE (Etienne), *ed.* North Munster studies: essays in commemoration of Monsignor Michael Moloney. Pp xvi, 535. Limerick: Thomond Archaeological Society, 1967.

128 WARE (*Sir* James). The whole works of Sir James Ware concerning Ireland, revised and improved . . . . Newly translated into English, revised and improved with many material additions and continued down to the beginning of the present century by Walter Harris. 2 vols. Dublin: Robert Bell; John Fleming, 1764.

> i. *The history of the bishops of that kingdom and such matters ecclesiastical and civil in which they were concerned, from the first propagation of Christianity therein to the present time.*
> ii. *The history and antiquities of Ireland; The history of the writers of Ireland.*
> Illustrated.

129 WATT (John Anthony), MORRALL (John Brimyard), MARTIN (Francis Xavier), *ed.* Medieval studies presented to Aubrey Gwynn, S.J. Pp xi, 509. Dublin: printed by Colm O Lochlainn at the Three Candles, 1961.

IV HISTORICAL GEOGRAPHY

(a) GENERAL

See also **384, 396.**

130 COMMON (Robert), *ed.* Northern Ireland from the air. Pp 104.
Belfast: Department of Geography, The Queen's University, 1964.
A photographic atlas, with commentary and line drawings. Includes
R. E. Glasscock, 'The past' (pp 36-55). Folding map. See also **654, 670.**

131 DEVITT (Matthew). The barony of Okethy. In *Kildare Arch. Soc.
Jn.*, viii (1915-17), 276-301, 388-98, 464-88.
Map; genealogical table.

132 EVANS (Emyr Estyn). The region and its parts. In *Belfast in its
regional setting* (1952), pp 15-28.
A useful geographical survey of Ulster.

133 FALKINER (Caesar Litton). The counties of Ireland: an historical
sketch of their origin, constitution, and gradual delimitation.
In *R.I.A. Proc.*, xxiv (1902-4), C, no. 11 (1903), 169-94.
Traces in detail the development of county organisation, including the
medieval liberties, relating it to the pre-Norman territorial divisions.

134 FLATRÈS (Pierre). Geographie rurale de quatre contrées celtiques:
Irlande, Galles, Cornwall & Man. Pp 618. Rennes: J. Plihon,
1957.
Includes an examination of the agricultural system, territorial divisions,
etc. of the pre-industrial Irish landscape, as revealed by the large-scale
maps of 19th century. See T. J. Hughes in *Ir. Geography*, iii (1954-8),
280-1.

135 FLATRÈS (Pierre). L'habitat agricole agglomére en Irlande. In
Chronique Geographique des Pays Celtes (Rennes), 1953, pp
112-24.

136 FREEMAN (Thomas Walter). Historical geography and the Irish
historian. In *I.H.S.*, v (1946-7), 139-46.
Stresses the importance of geography in the study of history and appeals
for efforts to reconstruct the map of Ireland at various stages in history.

137 FREEMAN (Thomas Walter). Ireland: its physical, historical, social
and economic geography. Pp xiv, 555. London: Methuen; New
York: Dutton, 1950; 2nd ed. *as* Ireland: a general and regional
geography. Pp xix, 556. 1960; 3rd ed. Pp xxx, 560. 1965; 4th ed.

Pp xix, 557, 1969; *Russian translation of 1st ed. as* Irlandiya: fizicheskaya i ekonomicheskaya geografiya. Sokrashchennyi perevod s angliiskogo L. M. Sapgir i R. R. Oberga. Redaktsyya i vstupitel'nyi stat'ya V. E. Kuninoi. Pp 399. Moscva: Izd-vo Ino-strannoi Lit-ry, 1952.

> Standard work, comprising a general survey followed by more detailed regional studies. Several maps, plates, diagrams, bibliographical notes.

138 GLASSCOCK (Robin Edgar). Ireland. In *Deserted medieval villages*, ed. M. W. Beresford and J. G. Hurst (London: Lutterworth P., 1971), pp 279-301.

> Ch. xi, 'The study of deserted medieval settlements (to 1968)' (pp 279-91). Ch. xii, 'Gazetteer of deserted towns, rural boroughs, and nucleated settlements'; 'Select bibliography' (pp. 292-301).

139 GLASSCOCK (Robin Edgar). Moated sites, and deserted boroughs and villages: two neglected aspects of Anglo-Norman settlement in Ireland. In *Irish geographical studies in honour of E. Estyn Evans*, ed. N. Stephens and R. E. Glasscock (Belfast: Department of Geography, The Queen's University, 1970), pp 162-77.

140 HOGAN (James). The tricha cét and related land-measures. In *R.I.A. Proc.*, xxxviii (1928-9), C, no. 7 (1929), 148-235.

> Examines its origins and development, and its relation to the Welsh cantref and Anglo-Norman cantred.

141 LEISTER (Ingeborg). Wald und Forst in Irland, unter besonderer Berücksichtigung der Grafschaft Tipperary. In *Erdkunde: Archiv für wissenschaftliche Geographie* (Bonn: Dümmlers), xvii (1963), 58-76.

> Includes 'Waldzerstörungen im Mittelalter' (p 60). English summary. Maps; photographs.

142 McCRACKEN (Eileen). The woodlands of Ireland, *circa* 1600. In *I.H.S.*, xi (1958-9), 271-96.

> A detailed description, based on documentary evidence and the subsequent location of ironworks. 2 maps.

143 MacIVOR (Dermot). The boundaries of Fir Rois, [by] Diarmuid Mac Iomhair. In *Louth Arch. Soc. Jn.*, xv (1961-4), 144-79.

> A reconstruction of the boundaries of the barony of Ardee, from documentary evidence. 3 maps. See also his 'The history of Fir Rois' in *Louth Arch. Soc. Jn.*, xv (1961-4), 321-48, with 3 maps.

144 O LOCHLAINN (Colm). Roadways in ancient Ireland. In *Féil-sgríbhinn Eóin Mhic Néill* (1940), pp 465-74.

> A preliminary report of his research into the Irish road system, *c.*450-1000. Map.

145 POWER (Patrick). The bounds and extent of Irish parishes. In *Féilscríbhinn Torna* (1947), pp 218-23.
A short explanation of the distinction between the civil and the ecclesiastical parish, and variations in names and boundaries over the centuries.

146 REEVES (William). On the townland distribution of Ireland. In *R.I.A. Proc.*, vii (1857-61), 473-90.
An analytical survey of the smaller territorial subdivisions, and some common elements in townland names, based on documentary evidence. Particularly useful for its explanation of local terminology.

(b) GAZETTEERS

See also **151-154**

147 KILLANIN (Michael Morris, 3rd Baron) *and* DUIGNAN (Michael Vincent). Shell guide to Ireland. Pp viii, 486. London: Ebury P., 1962; 2nd ed. Pp 512. 1967.
Alphabetical descriptive gazetteer, with emphasis on antiquities and items of historic or artistic interest. Historical introduction, short bibliography, glossaries, maps, 18 colour plates, many photographs. Lord Killanin is a former chairman of the National Monuments of Ireland Advisory Council, and Professor Duignan a leading archaeologist.

148 LEWIS (Samuel). A topographical dictionary of Ireland, comprising the several counties, cities, boroughs, corporate, market and post towns, parishes, and villages, with statistical descriptions .... 2 vols and atlas. London: S. Lewis, 1837; 2nd ed. 1842.
The gazetteer contains much interesting information on local history, but must be used cautiously on account of its age. *Lewis's atlas comprising the counties of Ireland and a general map of the kingdom* contains a map of each county, marking the barony boundaries before their reorganisation; these are very nearly as they were in medieval times.

(c) PLACE-NAMES

Only the more important or frequently cited works are listed here. Many specialised articles will be found in *R.S.A.I. Jn.*, **99**, and the local journals listed in Section II above; the older items should be used with great caution—see note on **159** below. See also **181**.

149 ARTHURS (John Brendan). Place-names. In *Belfast in its regional setting* (1952), pp 190-5.
Short historical account of Ulster place-names.

150 BULLETIN OF THE ULSTER PLACE-NAME SOCIETY. 5 vols. Belfast: The Society. 1952-7.
Edited by J. B. Arthurs (i.e. Seán MacAirt).

151 CENSUS OF IRELAND, 1851. General alphabetical index to the townlands and towns, parishes, and baronies of Ireland, showing the number of the sheet of the Ordnance Survey maps in which they appear. . . . Pp 12, 968. Dublin: Alex Thom. for H.M.S.O., 1861 (i.e. 1862). ([2942], H.C. 1862, li)
Introduction by William Donnelly (pp 3-12) headed: 'Census of Ireland. Townland index', by which title this and subsequent editions, **152, 153**, are generally known. Three separate indexes of townlands (pp 1-904), parishes (pp 905-57), and baronies (pp 958-68). An important manual for place-name study.

152 CENSUS OF IRELAND, 1871. Alphabetical index to the townlands and towns of Ireland, showing the number of the sheet of the Ordnance Survey maps on which they appear. . . . Pp [4], 799. Dublin: H.M.S.O., 1877. ([C 1711], H.C. 1877, lxxxvii)
See **151**.

153 CENSUS OF IRELAND, 1901. General topographical index . . . . Pp xi, 1049. Dublin: H.M.S.O., 1904. ([Cd 2071], H.C. 1904, cix)
See **151, 154**.

154 CENSUS OF IRELAND, 1911. Supplement to the General topographical index of Ireland, containing all the territorial divisions in which alteration has been made between 31st March 1901 and 2nd April 1911. . . . Pp [2], 42. London: H.M.S.O., 1913. ([Cd 6756], H.C. 1913, lxxx, 1-44)
Supplement to **153**.

155 THE CIVIL SURVEY, A.D. 1654-1656. [Edited] by Robert C. Simington. 10 vols. Dublin: Stationery Office, 1931-61. (I.M.C.)
Includes many place-names no longer in use.

156 DINNSEANCHAS. Baile Átha Cliath: An Cumann Logainmneacha, 1964- .
Journal of the society, now the most important single source for the study of place-names in Ireland. Most articles in Irish. Includes 'Foilseacháin, 1964- ', annual lists of publications relating to place-names.

157 GOBLET (Yann Morvan). A topographical index of the parishes and townlands of Ireland in Sir William Petty's MSS barony maps, c.1655-9 (Bibliothèque nationale de Paris, Fonds anglais, nos 1 & 2), and Hiberniae delineatio, c.1672. Collected and edited by Y. M. Goblet. Pp xx, 379. Dublin: Stationery Office, 1932. (I.M.C.)
2,000 parish and 25,000 townland names, giving spellings in both sources. See also **188, 189.**

158 HOGAN (Edmund Ignatius). Onomasticon Goedelicum locorum et tribum hiberniae et scotiae: an index, with identifications, to the Gaelic names of places and tribes. Pp xvi, 696. Dublin: Hodges, Figgis; London: Williams & Norgate, 1910.
Published under the auspices of R.I.A. A basic pioneer work of serious scholarship. Mainly pre-Norman, but useful for identifying Irish place-names. Map.

159 JOYCE (Patrick Weston). The origin and history of Irish names of places. 3 vols. Dublin: McGlashan & Gill, 1869-1913.
Various editions of vols i-ii, which discuss origins; vol. iii is an alphabetical list of names with explanations. The work predates the disciplined study of the subject, and many of the explanations are speculative translations since refuted by examination of documentary evidence for earlier forms.

160 MACNEILL (Eoin). Our place-names. In *R.S.A.I. Jn.,* lxviii (1938), 189-95.
A useful introduction.

161 Ó FOGHLUDHA (Risteárd). Log-ainmneacha .i. Dictionary of Irish placenames (7,000): English-Gaelic. Pp [4], 80. [Baile Átha Cliath]: Brún agus Ó Nualláin, [1935].
Alphabetical list of provinces, counties, dioceses, baronies, electoral divisions, post-offices, rivers, mountains, lochs, islands, etc., with Irish equivalents.

162 Ó MÁILLE (Thomás S.). Place names from Galway documents. In *Galway Arch. Soc. Jn.,* xxiii (1948-9), 93-137; xxiv (1950-51), 58-70, 130-55.—Four County Galway place names. In *Galway Arch. Soc. Jn.,* xxv (1952-4), 28-31.—County Galway place names. In *Galway Arch. Soc. Jn.,* xxv (1952-4), 81-5.—Five County Galway placenames. In *Galway Arch. Soc. Jn.,* xxviii (1958-9), 12-17.

163 OTWAY-RUTHVEN (Annette Jocelyn). Place-names in Ireland. In *Ir. Geography*, ii (1949-53), 45-51.

Examines the materials and problems of place-name study. 2 maps.

164 POKORNY (Julius). Zur Anglisierung irischer Orts- und Flussnamen. In *Beiträge zur Namenforschung* (Heidelberg: C. Winter), iii (1951-2), 89-91. (Zu keltischen Namen, 8)

165 POWER (Patrick). Place-names and antiquities of S.E. Cork. In *R.I.A. Proc.*, xxxiv (1917-19), C, no. 1 (1917), 1-32; no. 9 (1918), 184-230; xxxvi (1921-4), C, no. 11 (1923), 164-205.

166 POWER (Patrick). The place names of Decies. Pp xxvii, 503. London: D. Nutt, 1907; 2nd ed. Pp [ix], 489. Cork: Cork U.P.; Oxford: Blackwell, 1952.

At head of title: Log-ainmneacha na nDeise.
Also published serially in *Waterford Arch. Soc. Jn.*, ix (1906)-xii (1909).

167 PRICE (Liam). The need for a study of Irish place names. In *N. Munster Antiq. Jn.*, i (1936-9), 29-33.

Some important general observations, forming a useful introduction to the subject.

167a PRICE (Liam). A note on the use of the word *baile* in placenames. In *Celtica*, vi (1963), 119-24.

168 PRICE (Liam). On the distribution of place-names beginning with Dun-, Lis-, and Rath-. In *R.S.A.I. Jn.*, lxxxviii (1958), 83-4.

A short note and table showing the distribution of these elements in the townland-names of each county and province. Based on an analysis of the 'Townland index', **151**.

169 PRICE (Liam). Place-name study as applied to history. In *R.S.A.I. Jn.*, lxxix (1949), 26-38.

Three detailed examples.

170 PRICE (Liam). The place-names of Co. Wicklow. Pp xcvi, 532. Dublin: Institute for Advanced Studies, 1945-67.

Published in 7 fascs, covering the whole county. Fasc. 7 contains introduction and index, with shortened versions of his earlier papers: 'The place-names of the barony of Arklow, county of Wicklow: their early forms collected' in *R.I.A. Proc.*, xlvi (1941), C, no. 5, pp 237-86; 'The place-names of the barony of Newcastle, county of Wicklow: their early forms collected' in *R.I.A. Proc.*, xliv (1937-8), C, no. 6 (1938), 139-79. These must still be referred to for lists of spellings and detailed notes.

171 WALSH (Paul). The placenames of Westmeath. Pp xxxv, 402. Dublin: Institute for Advanced Studies, 1957.

Edited by Colm O Lochlainn. Pt 1 originally published as *The place-names of Westmeath. Pt 1. The Ordnance Survey letters referring to the county*, abridged and edited by P. Walsh (pp viii, 116, Dublin: the editor, 1915). This transcribes the relevant letters of John O Donovan and Thomas O Conor, 1837. Pt 2 lists place-names by barony, with the author's uncompleted notes for some baronies as an appendix. The introduction (pp ix-xxxv) is a lecture, 'Ancient Westmeath', delivered in 1938, containing a short history of the county and the older land-areas now contained in it.

(d) CARTOGRAPHY

(i) General

172 ANDREWS (John Harwood). Ireland in maps: an introduction; with a catalogue of an exhibition mounted in the Library of Trinity College, Dublin, 1961, by the Geographical Society of Ireland in conjunction with the Ordnance Survey of Ireland. Pp 36. Dublin: Dolmen P., 1961.
A useful historical introduction and handbook.

173 ANDREWS (John Harwood). 'Ireland in maps': a bibliographical postscript. In *Ir. Geography*, iv (1959-63), 234-43.
Important, detailed review of Irish cartobibliographical material to 1824. Notes (pp 239-43) constitute a bibliography of Irish cartography before the Ordnance Survey.

174 ANDREWS (Michael Corbet). The map of Ireland, A.D. 1300-1700. In *Belfast Natur. Hist. Soc. Proc.*, 1922-3, pp 9-33.
Surveys the development of the cartography of Ireland from Ptolemy to Petty. 6 plates of early maps. See also W. A. McComish, 'Early maps of Ireland in the Andrews collection of the Royal Geographical Society' in *The Geographical Journal* (London: Royal Geographical Society), cxxxiv (1968), 306-8.

175 HARDINGE (William Henry). On manuscript mapped townland surveys in Ireland of a public character, from their introduction to 23rd October 1641. In *R.I.A. Proc.*, viii (1861-4), 39-55.

176 LOWRY-CORRY (Somerset Richard), *4th Earl Belmore*. The Irish historical atlas, 1609. In his *Descriptive notes on The Irish historical atlas, 1609; the old castles of County Tyrone; James Spottiswoode, Bishop of Clogher, 1621-1644; the old Enniskillen vestry book, 1666-1797; with some notes from the parish registers of St Michan's, Dublin, and of Derryvullen* (Belfast: McCaw, Stevenson & Orr, 1903. *U.J.A.*, new ser., Special vol.), pp 1-32.
A detailed description of **185**, with tracings of 8 maps, and other illustrations.

177 MACNEILL (Niall). The Ordnance Survey of Ireland. In *Administration* (Dublin: Institute of Public Administration), xiv (1966), 1-19.
A historical account.

178 MADDEN (P. G.). The Ordnance Survey of Ireland. In *Ir. Sword*, v (1961-2), 155-63.
A history from its inception in 1824, with a list of previous surveys in Ireland, c.1560-1820.

179 ORDNANCE SURVEY OF IRELAND. Catalogue of the large-scale maps, with dates of survey and latest revision shown on the indexes to each county . . . . 26 maps. Dublin: Stationery Office, 1964.

180 ORDNANCE SURVEY OF IRELAND. Catalogue of the maps and other publications of the Ordnance Survey, 30th June, 1946. Pp 42; 4 maps. Dublin: Stationery Office, 1946.
Includes dates of surveys and revisions.

181 WESTROPP (Thomas Johnson). Early Italian maps of Ireland. In *R.I.A. Proc.*, xxx (1912-13), C, no. 16 (1913), 361-428.
An account of the Portolan charts and of the Hiberno-Italian commercial relations leading to their production in 14th-15th centuries. It is also an important contribution to economic history, especially the wine trade, with sections on 'Commerce and foreign merchants after 1170' (pp 376-90), 'The Irish ports on the maps' (pp 390-402), 'The customs' (pp 402-5), 'Irish shipping' (p 405). 'The place-names, 1300-1600' (pp 411-26) should also be noted. 10 maps. See also G. H. Orpen, 'Ptolemy's map of Ireland' in *R.S.A.I. Jn.*, xxiv (1894), 115-28.

(ii) Maps

182 HADCOCK (Richard Neville). Monastic Ireland. Scale 1:625,000, or 1 inch to 9.86 miles. Dublin: Ordnance Survey Office, 1960; 2nd ed. 1965.
Published with a pamphlet (pp 25; 2nd ed.,ᶠpp 30) containing a historical introduction by Aubrey Gwynn and an index of houses shown on the map. Also issued folded and bound with the pamphlet, with cover title: *Map of monastic Ireland*.
A distribution map showing the sites of all known religious houses, *c*. 450-1600, with a descriptive symbol for each type. The National Grid, main contours, modern roads and railways are overprinted faintly. Reconstructed 15th-16th-century diocesan boundaries are also shown. See also **432**.

183 HAYES-MCCOY (Gerard Anthony), *ed.* Ulster and other Irish maps, *c*.1600. Pp xv, 36; 23 maps. Dublin: Stationery Office, 1964. (I.M.C.)
Facsimile of N.L.I. MS 2656, affording valuable information on houses, fortifications, etc. in various localities. May be used with caution for the later middle ages. See also K. Danaher, **647**.

184 JOHNSTON (Robert). [Superimposition of the Down Survey on Townland maps. Scale *c*.3½ inches to 1 mile. Dublin: I.M.C., 1954- .]
Photocopies of a manuscript reconstruction of the Down Survey (1655-8) on 1st ed. of O.S. (1837-46), **186**. Original deposited in N.L.I. Incomplete at compiler's death. Should be used cautiously as disparity between Down Survey and O.S. boundaries generally indicates inaccuracy in the Down Survey rather than actual change.

185 ORDNANCE SURVEY. Maps of the escheated counties in Ireland, 1609. Copied at the Ordnance Survey Office, Southampton. Pp 2; 31 maps. Southampton: Ordnance Survey, 1861.

Preface by Hans C. Hamilton. Commonly known as 'The Irish historical atlas'. For a detailed description see S. R. Lowry-Corry, 176.

186 ORDNANCE SURVEY OF IRELAND. Townland survey. Scale 1:10,560, or 6 inches to 1 mile. *c.*1900 maps. Dublin: Ordnance Survey, 1837-46.

1st ed. shows barony and civil parish boundaries approximately as they were in medieval times, before the adjustments shown on later revisions. *Index* (Scale 1:126,720 or ½ inch to 1 mile; some sheets ¼ inch to 1 mile. 32 maps) also shows civil parish boundaries.

187 ORDNANCE SURVEY OF IRELAND, SHOWING COUNTY BOUNDARIES [AND] BARONY BOUNDARIES. Scale 1:633,600, or 1 inch to 10 miles. Dublin: Ordnance Survey Office, 1938.

Known as 'The barony map'. A useful guide for the medieval baronies, but should be used in conjunction with *Lewis's atlas*, **148**, and the *Townland survey*, **186**, as many boundaries were altered in the later 19th century.

188 PETTY (*Sir* William). Hibernia regnum. Scale 1 inch to 320 perches, [or 1:62,360]. 2 vols. Southampton: Ordnance Survey, 1908.

Barony maps, showing parish and townland boundaries, reproduced from the Down Survey (1655-8) maps in the Bibliothèque nationale. Incomplete. Some copies have boundaries hand-coloured. See Seán Ó Domhnaill, 'The maps of the Down Survey' in *I.H.S.*, iii (1942-3), 381-92.

189 PETTY (*Sir* William). Hiberniae delineatio quoad hactenus licuit perfectissima studio Guilelmi Petty. Pp [4]; 36 maps. [London, 1685]; 2nd ed. [Dublin]: G. Grierson, [*c.*1734]; *reprint of 1685 ed. as* Hiberniae delineatio: atlas of Ireland. Newcastle-upon-Tyne: Frank Graham, 1968; *repr., with a critical introduction by J. H. Andrews.* Shannon: Irish U.P., 1970.

V GENERAL HISTORY

(a) GENERAL HISTORIES

190 BECKETT (James Camlin). A short history of Ireland. Pp viii, 208. London: Hutchinson, 1952. (Hutchinson's University Library, History Series); 2nd ed. 1958; 3rd ed. Pp 191. 1966.

> Ch. i gives a concise account of the period to *c*.1500. Short bibliography; 2 maps.

191 CURTIS (Edmund). A history of Ireland. Pp xi, 434. London: Methuen, 1936; 4th ed., revised. 1943; 6th ed. 1950.

> Pp 47-167 cover the period 1166-1540. Short bibliography; 4 maps relating to the medieval period. Cf. **199**.

192 DUNLOP (Robert). Ireland from the earliest times to the present day. Pp 224. London: Oxford U.P., 1922.

> 'The Anglo-Irish colony, 1169-1541' (pp 27-65) remains a good introductory survey.

193 LELAND (Thomas). The history of Ireland from the invasion of Henry II; with a preliminary discourse on the antient state of that kingdom. 3 vols. Dublin: R. Moncrieffe, 1773; 2nd ed. London: J. Nourse; G. Robinson, 1773; 3rd ed. Dublin, 1774; *repr.* Dublin: printed by B. Smith, 1814; *French translation by Marc Antoine Eidous as* Histoire d'Irlande depuis l'invasion d'Henri II; avec un discours préliminaire sur l'ancien état de ce royaume. 7 vols. Maestricht: Jean-Edme Dufour & Phil. Roux, 1779.

194 MOODY (Theodore William) *and* MARTIN (Francis Xavier), *ed.* The course of Irish history. Pp 404. Cork: Mercier P., 1967; New York: Weybright & Talley, [1967].

> A chronological survey originally written as script for a television series broadcast by R.T.E., 1966, consisting of independent chapters by specialists, each concentrating on a particular aspect of his period. Valuable as an introduction, but not a textbook. Includes F. X. Martin, 'The Anglo-Norman invasion, 1169-*c*.1300' (pp 123-43); J. F. Lydon, 'The medieval English colony, *c*.1300-*c*.1400' (pp 144-57); Art Cosgrove, 'The Gaelic resurgence and the Geraldine supremacy, *c*.1400-1534' (pp 158-73). Copiously illustrated with photographs and facsimiles. Bibliography, chronological table, maps.

195 SHILLMAN (Bernard). A short history of the Jews in Ireland. Pp [8], 151. Dublin: printed by Cahill for private distribution by Eason, 1945.

> Includes a very short survey of the pre-Cromwellian period (pp 9-12).

(b) MEDIEVAL PERIOD

196 BROOKS (Eric St John). Knights' fees in counties Wexford, Carlow and Kilkenny, 13th-15th century; with commentary. Pp xiv, 306. Dublin: Stationery Office, 1950. (I.M.C.)

> A detailed analysis of the subinfeudation of the area and of the devolution of the various fees after the partition of Leinster in 1247. See also J. Otway-Ruthven, **212**.

197 CAHILL (Edward). Ireland in the Anglo-Norman period, 1170-1540. In *I.E.R.*, 5th ser., xlviii (1936), 142-60.

198 CAHILL (Edward). The political state of mediaeval Ireland. In *I.E.R.*, 5th ser., xxv (1925), 245-65.

> An account of the main political groups—native Irish, Anglo-Norman lords, English colonists—and a comparison with the Moorish invasion of Spain.

199 CURTIS (Edmund). A history of mediaeval Ireland from 1110 to 1513. Pp vi, 436. Dublin: Maunsel & Roberts, 1923; *repr.*, Dublin, Cork: Talbot P., 1927; 2nd ed. *as* A history of medieval Ireland from 1086 to 1513. Pp xxxv, 433. London: Methuen, 1938; *repr.*, New York: Barnes & Noble; London: Methuen, 1968. (Methuen Library Reprints); *Irish translation as* Stair na hÉireann sa mheánaois, 1086-1513, Éamonn Cuirteis do scríobh. Tomás de Bhial do chuir Gaeilge air. Pp xxxi, 506. Baile Átha Cliath: Oifig an tSoláthair, 1956.

> Standard work, now largely superseded by A. J. Otway-Ruthven, **211**. 2nd ed. should be used as the work was completely rewritten, but reference is sometimes made to 1st ed. for detail. Appendices on Ostmen, towns, legal treatment of the Irish; pedigrees of chief families; 3 maps. For criticism, see A. Gwynn in *Hist. Studies*, i (1958), 98-9; H. G. Richardson, 'English institutions in medieval Ireland' in *I.H.S.*, i (1938-9), 382-92.

200 DAVIES (*Sir* John). A discoverie of the true causes why Ireland was never entirely subdued nor brought under obedience of the crowne of England untill the beginning of his Maiesties happie raigne. Pp 287. [London]: John Jaggard, 1612.

> Many later editions and reprints, the most accessible being in *Ireland under Elizabeth and James the First*, ed. Henry Morley (London: Routledge, 1890. The Carisbrooke Library, 10), pp 213-342. Mainly important for the documents cited.

201 GILBERT (*Sir* John Thomas). A history of the viceroys of Ireland; with notices of the castle of Dublin and its chief occupants in former times. Pp xxxvi, 613. Dublin, London: James Duffy, 1865.

Sets the chief governors in historical context, from 1166 to 1509, using original documents, many of which have since been destroyed.

202 HENNIG (John). Medieval Ireland in Cistercian records. In *I.E.R.*, 5th ser., lxxiii (1950), 226-42.

An examination of the evidence published in *Statuta Capitulorum Generalium Ordinis Cisterciensis, ab anno 1116 ad annum 1786*, ed. Joseph M. Canivez (8 vols, Louvain: Revue d'histoire ecclésiastique, 1933-41. Bibliothèque de la Revue d'Histoire Ecclésiastique, fascs 9-14, 14A, 14B).

203 LYNCH (William). A view of the legal institutions, honorary hereditary offices, and feudal baronies established in Ireland during the reign of Henry the Second; deduced from court rolls, inquisitions and other original records. Pp xxiv, 360. London: Longman, Rees, Orme, Brown & Green, 1830.

Traces the development of feudal and administrative institutions during the middle ages, citing sources since destroyed.

204 MACNEILL (Eoin). Phases of Irish history. Pp [7], 364. Dublin: Gill, 1919; *repr.* 1968.

An important series of public lectures, mainly on the pre-Norman period but including 'Medieval Irish institutions' (pp 274-99); 'The Norman conquest' (pp 300-22); 'The Irish rally' (pp 323-56). See review by Arthur E. Clery in *Studies*, viii (1919), 654-7.

205 Ó CORRÁIN (Donncha). Celts and Normans, [by] Gearóid Mac-Gearailt [*pseud.*]. Pp [7], 184. Dublin: Gill & Macmillan, 1969. (A History of Ireland; general editor, Margaret MacCurtain)

School textbook, but superbly illustrated.

206 ORPEN (Goddard Henry). The effects of Norman rule in Ireland, 1169-1333. In *A.H.R.*, xix (1913-14), 245-56.

Paper read at the International Congress of Historical Studies, London, 1913, containing a concise account of social developments. Subsequent research has shown the beneficial aspects to be somewhat overstated.

207 ORPEN (Goddard Henry). Ireland, 1315-c.1485. In *The Cambridge medieval history*, viii (Cambridge: Cambridge U.P., 1936), pp 450-65.

Short narrative account, following **208**.

208 ORPEN (Goddard Henry). Ireland to 1315. In *The Cambridge medieval history*, vii (Cambridge: Cambridge U.P., 1932), pp 527-47.

Accompanying map: 'Ireland after the Norman invasion'. See also **207**.

209 ORPEN (Goddard Henry). Ireland under the Normans, 1169-1333. 4 vols. Oxford: Clarendon P., 1911-20; *repr.*, 1968.

Remains the best account of the period. In need of correction on some points, but includes much detailed information not otherwise accessible. Maps; genealogical tables. No cumulative index, but vols i-ii are indexed in vol. ii, and vols iii-iv in vol. iv, which also contains 'Addenda et corrigenda to volumes i and ii'. For a recent reassessment, see J. Otway-Ruthven in *I.H.S.*, xvi (1968-9), 501-2.

210 ORPEN (Goddard Henry). The Normans in Tirowen and Tirconnell. In *R.S.A.I. Jn.*, xlv (1915), 275-88.

A comprehensive account of Anglo-Norman efforts to control the region prior to 1333.

211 OTWAY-RUTHVEN (Annette Jocelyn). A history of medieval Ireland. With an introduction by Kathleen Hughes. Pp xv, 454. London: Benn; New York: Barnes & Noble, 1968.

Indispensable companion to all studies of the period from the 12th century to 1494, correcting and supplementing earlier works on many matters. Basically a narrative account, with important chapters on social, ecclesiastical and administrative institutions. Detailed references; excellent maps; bibliography. See A. Gwynn, 'The history of medieval Ireland' in *Studies*, lvii (1968), 161-73; J. F. Lydon in *I.H.S.*, xvii (1970-1), 123-8; Donald W. Sutherland in *Speculum*, xliv (1969), 648-50.

212 OTWAY-RUTHVEN (Annette Jocelyn). Knights' fees in Kildare, Leix and Offaly. In *R.S.A.I. Jn.*, xci (1961), 163-81.

An analysis of the subinfeudation of the area, based mainly on 14th-century inquisitions and pipe rolls. Map. Cf. E. St J. Brooks, **196**.

213 SAYLES (George Osborne). Medieval [Ulster]. In *Belfast in its regional setting* (1952), pp 98-103.

Short historical survey.

(c) ANGLO-NORMAN INVASION AND SETTLEMENT, 1170-1216

214 BLAKE (Martin Joseph). William de Burgh: progenitor of the Burkes in Ireland. In *Galway Arch. Soc. Jn.*, vii (1911-12), 83-101; *repr. with revisions.* Pp 20. Galway: O'Gorman, 1911.
Cf. G. H. Orpen, **267.**

215 DUNNING (Patrick Joseph). Pope Innocent III and the Irish kings. In *Jn. Eccles. Hist.*, viii (1957), 17-32.
Examines Innocent's attitude to the Gaelic kings and their relations with John and the Anglo-Norman lords.

216 EDWARDS (Robert Walter Dudley). Anglo-Norman relations with Connacht, 1169-1224. In *I.H.S.*, i (1938-9), 135-53.
Narrates the attempts to wrest the powers of kingship from the O'Connors.

217 GOGARTY (Thomas). Gilla Mic Liag Mac Ruaidhri, primate of Armagh, 1137-1174. In *I.E.R.*, 5th ser., xi (1918), 133-49; xii (1918), 121-39.
Gelasius MacRory.

218 GWYNN (Aubrey Osborn). Archbishop John Cumin. In *Reportorium Novum*, i (1955-6), 285-310.

219 GWYNN (Aubrey Osborn). Armagh and Louth in the 12th and 13th centuries. In *Seanchas Ardmhacha*, i (1954-5), no. 1 (1954), 1-11; no. 2 (1955), 17-37.
Pt 2 covers the period of Norman settlement.

220 GWYNN (Aubrey Osborn). Saint Lawrence O'Toole as legate in Ireland, 1179-1180. In *Anal. Bolland.*, lxviii (1950), 223-40; also published as *Extraits des Anal. Bolland.*, 817.
An examination of the last year of his life, in the context of ecclesiastical reform, Anglo-Norman settlement, and animosity towards him from both Henry II and native Irish elements, especially in the province of Armagh.

221 LEGRIS (Albert). Saint Laurent O'Toole, archevêque de Dublin. Pp 31. Eu: R. Odic, 1908.
Brief account of his later years.

222 LEGRIS (Albert). Saint Laurent O'Toole (Saint Laurent d'Eu), archevêque de Dublin, 1128-1180. Pp ix, 152. Rouen: G. Cacheux; Eu: Largouet, 1914; *English translation as* Life of St Laurence O'Toole, archbishop of Dublin, 1128-1180. Pp x, 118. Dublin: Catholic Truth Society of Ireland, 1914.

Biography, with a bibliography discussing the 13th-century vitae and listing other published biographies.

223 LYNCH (John). Cambrensis eversus, seu potius historica fides in rebus hibernicis Giraldo Cambrensi abrogata; in quo plerasque justi historici dotes desiderari, plerosque naevos inesse, ostendit Gratianus Lucius, hibernas, qui etiam aliquot res memorabiles hibernicas veteris et novae memoriae passim e re nata huic operi inseruit. Impress. an. MDCLXII. Edited with translation and notes by Matthew Kelly. 3 vols. Dublin: Celtic Society, 1848-52.

Also issued to members of the Irish Archaeological Society, 1853.
An attack on Giraldus Cambrensis from the 17th-century Gaelic standpoint. See also **224, 235**.

224 MARTIN (Francis Xavier). Gerald of Wales, Norman reporter on Ireland. In *Studies*, lviii (1969), 279-92.

An account of the visits of Giraldus Cambrensis to Ireland in 1183 and 1185 and his reports thereon in his *Topographia Hibernica* and *Expugnatio Hibernica*. Also refers to earlier biographical writings on Giraldus. See also F. M. Powicke, **235**.

225 MILLS (James). The Norman settlement in Leinster: the cantreds near Dublin. In *R.S.A.I. Jn.*, xxiv (1894), 160-75.

Analyses the subinfeudation of the area reserved from the grant of Leinster to Strongbow.

226 NORGATE (Kate). The bull Laudabiliter. In *E.H.R.*, vii (1893), 18-52.

Includes a review of the controversy to date. See also **230, 240-43**.

227 O'DOHERTY (John Francis). The Anglo-Norman invasion, 1167-71. In *I.H.S.*, i (1938-9), 154-7. (Historical Revision, iii)

A concise résumé of events prior to the arrival of Henry II.

228 O'DOHERTY (John Francis). Historical criticism of the 'Song of Dermot and the Earl'. In *I.H.S.*, i (1938-9), 4-20; Correspondence, *ibid.*, pp 294-6.

Disagreement with Orpen on the use of the 'Song' as historical evidence.

229 O'DOHERTY (John Francis). Laurentius von Dublin und das irische Normannentum. Pp 96. München: Druck von Kastner u. Callwey, 1933. (Inaugural-Dissertation zur Erlangung der Doktorwürde der Philosophischen Fakultät, ı. Sektion, der Ludwig-Maximilians-Universität zu München); *English translation as* St Lawrence O'Toole and the Anglo-Norman invasion. In *I.E.R.*, 5th ser., 1 (1937), 449-77, 600-25; li (1938), 131-46.

> The best account of Anglo-Norman expansion, 1167-80, with special reference to the church. Based on a careful study of the sources, and professing an impartiality lacking in Orpen. English version omits footnotes and references.

230 O'DOHERTY (John Francis). Rome and the Anglo-Norman invasion of Ireland. In *I.E.R.*, 5th ser., xlii (1933), 131-45.

231 ORPEN (Goddard Henry). The battle of Dundonnell (Baginbun), A.D. 1170. In *R.S.A.I. Jn.*, xxxiv (1904), 354-60.

> A reconstructed account of the battle, with corroborative evidence for his identification of the site in **232**.

232 ORPEN (Goddard Henry). Site of Raymond's fort, Dundunnolf, Baginbun. In *R.S.A.I. Jn.*, xxviii (1898), 155-60.

> See also **231**.

233 OTWAY-RUTHVEN (Annette Jocelyn). The character of Norman settlement in Ireland. In *Hist. Studies*, v (1965), 75-84.

> A descriptive survey of the nature of the settlement and the ensuing territorial structure, with a detailed analysis of the racial and social composition of the settlers.

234 POOLE (Austin Lane). From Domesday Book to Magna Carta, 1087-1216. Pp xvi, 541. Oxford: Clarendon P., 1951. (The Oxford History of England, iii); 2nd ed. 1955.

> 'Ireland' (pp 302-17). Short narrative bibliography (pp 509-10).

235 POWICKE (*Sir* Frederick Maurice). Gerald of Wales. In *John Rylands Lib. Bull.*, xii (1928), 389-410; repr. in his *The Christian life in the middle ages, and other essays* (Oxford: Clarendon P., 1935; repr., 1966), pp 107-29.

> A biographical study, See also F. X. Martin, **224**.

236 RICHARDSON (Henry Gerald). Norman Ireland in 1212. In *I.H.S.*, iii (1942-3), 144-58.

> Review of *The Irish pipe roll of 14 John, 1211-1212*, **364**, surveying its evidence on Irish administration, etc., with special reference to William Marshall. Includes corrections to the published text (pp 155-7) and an additional note by Aubrey Gwynn (pp 157-8); these have subsequently been incorporated in the editors' corrigenda.

237 ROBINSON (Joseph Armitage). The early career of John Cumin, archbishop of Dublin. In his *Somerset historical essays* (London: Oxford U.P. for the British Academy, 1921), pp 90-9.
Printed as an appendix to his paper 'Early Somerset archdeacons'.

237a ROCHE (Richard). The Norman invasion of Ireland. Pp 134. Tralee: Anvil Books, 1970.
A factual short account. See also *The Norman invasion of Ireland*, ed. F. X. Martin (London: Methuen; New York: Cornell U.P.), broadcast as Thomas Davis lectures in 1969, to be published in 1971.

238 RONAN (Myles Vincent). St Laurentius, archbishop of Dublin: original testimonies for canonization. In *I.E.R.*, 5th ser., xxvii (1926), 347-64; xxviii (1926), 247-56, 467-80.
Commentary on the documents recommending his canonisation in 1226.

239 ROUND (John Horace). The conquest of Ireland. In his *The commune of London, and other studies* (Westminster: Constable, 1899), pp 137-70.
Of interest mainly as a discussion of *The song of Dermot and the Earl*, ed. G. H. Orpen (Oxford: Clarendon P., 1892), marred somewhat by the intrusion of the author's political sentiments.

240 ROUND (John Horace). The Pope and the conquest of Ireland. In his *The commune of London, and other studies* (Westminster: Constable, 1899), pp 171-200.
Includes criticism of other late 19th-century contributions to the Laudabiliter controversy. See also **226, 242**.

241 SCHEFFER-BOICHORST (Paul). Hat Papst Hadrian IV. zu Gunsten des englischen Königs über Irland verfügt? In *Mittheilungen des Instituts für Oesterreichische Geschichtsforschung*, Ergänzungsband iv (Innsbruck: Verlag der Wagner'schen Universitäts-Buchhandlung, 1893), pp 101-22.
Part ii of his 'Zwei Untersuchungen zur Geschichte der päpstlichen Territorial- und Finanzpolitik'. See note on **242**.

242 SHEEHY (Maurice Patrick Joseph). The bull Laudabiliter: a problem in medieval diplomatique and history. In *Galway Arch. Soc. Jn.*, xxix (1960-1), 45-70.
A historiographical survey and critical reassessment, with a bibliography of the more important contributions since 1556.

243 THATCHER (Oliver Joseph). Studies concerning Adrian IV. In *Decennial Publications of the University of Chicago*, 1st ser., iv (1903), 153-238.
Includes discussion of Laudabiliter (pp 153-78).

244 WARREN (Wilfred Lewis). The interpretation of twelfth-century Irish history. In *Hist. Studies*, vii (1969), 1-19.

A stimulating reassessment of the significance of events in Ireland, considered in their European context.

245 WARREN (Wilfred Lewis). Ireland in the twelfth century. In *I.C.H.S, Bull.*, new ser., ix (1962-3), nos 96-97 (Summer-Autumn 1962), pp 2-3.

A summary discussion of the significance of the Anglo-Norman invasions and Hildebrandine reforms in ending Irish isolation. See also **244**.

246 WATT (John Anthony). Laudabiliter in medieval diplomacy and propaganda. In *I.E.R.*, 5th ser., lxxxvii (1957), 420-32.

The use of the Bull in subsequent diplomatic history, 12th-15th centuries. See also **242**.

(d) THE THIRTEENTH CENTURY, 1216-1315

247 BROOKS (Eric St John). Archbishop Henry of London and his Irish connections. In *R.S.A.I. Jn.*, lx (1930), 1-22.
Henry Blund's relatives in Ireland.

248 CROWE (Michael Bertram). Peter of Ireland: Aquinas's teacher of the artes liberales. In *Arts libéraux et philosophie au moyen age: actes du quatrième Congrès international de philosophie médiévale, Université de Montréal, Montréal, Canada, 27 août-2 septembre 1967* (Montréal: Institut d'études médiévales; Paris: Librairie philosophique J. Vrin, 1969), pp 619-26.
A preliminary investigation, drawing some tentative conclusions on his career. Other works are referred to in footnotes, but see also **249, 250**.

249 CROWE (Michael Bertram). Peter of Ireland: teacher of St Thomas Aquinas. In *Studies*, xlv (1956), 443-56.
See also **248**, which covers similar ground.

250 CROWE (Michael Bertram). Peter of Ireland's approach to metaphysics. In *Die Metaphysik im Mittelalter: ihr Ursprung und ihre Bedeutung: Vorträge des II. Internationalen Kongresses für Mittelalterliche Philosophie, Köln, 31. August-6. September 1961*, im Auftrage der Société internationale pour l'étude de la philosophie médiévale (S.I.E.P.M.), hrsg. von Paul Wilpert, unter Mitarbeit von Willehad Paul Eckert (Berlin: De Gruyter, 1963. Miscellanea Mediaevalia: Veröffentlichungen des Thomas-Instituts an der Universität Köln, Bd 2), pp 154-60.

251 CURTIS (Edmund). Sheriff's accounts for County Tipperary, 1275-6. In *R.I.A. Proc.*, xlii (1934-5), C, no. 5 (1934), 65-95.
Includes commentary. Additional notes by G. H. Orpen (pp 92-5).

252 CURTIS (Edmund). The Wars of Turlogh: an historical document. In *The Irish Review: a monthly magazine of Irish literature, art & science* (Dublin: Irish Review Publishing Co.), ii (1912-13), 577-86, 644-7; iii (1913-14), 34-41.
A good popular account of the de Clare-O'Brien struggles in Thomond, 1275-1345, based on the 14th-century 'Caithréim Thoirdhealbhaigh'. See also L. F. McNamara, **263**, and T. J. Westropp, **277, 278**.

253 EDWARDS (Robert Walter Dudley). 'Magna Carta Hiberniae'. In *Féil-sgríbhinn Eóin Mhic Néill* (1940), pp 307-18.
An examination of the evidence for independent issues of Magna Carta in Ireland. See also H. G. Richardson, **273**.

254 GWYNN (Aubrey Osborn). Henry of London, archbishop of Dublin: a study in Anglo-Norman statecraft. In *Studies*, xxxviii (1949), 297-306, 389-402.

His career as archbishop and justiciar, 1213-24, and his campaign to establish an English hierarchy in the Irish church, See also E. St J. Brooks, **247**.

255 GWYNN (Aubrey Osborn). Nicholas Mac Maol Íosa, archbishop of Armagh, 1272-1303. In *Féil-sgríbhinn Eóin Mhic Néill* (1940), pp 394-405.

A biographical sketch of a vigorous opponent of Anglo-Norman officialdom, perhaps over-emphasising the racial aspect.

256 KNOX (Hubert Thomas). Occupation of Connaught by the Anglo-Normans after A.D. 1237. In *R.S.A.I. Jn.*, xxxii (1902), 132-8, 393-406; xxxiii (1903), 58-74, 179-89, 284-94.

Mainly a commentary on the inquisitions of 1333. See also **257**.

257 KNOX (Hubert Thomas). Occupation of the county of Galway by the Anglo-Normans after 1237. In *R.S.A.I. Jn.*, xxxi (1901), 365-70.

A summary of the subinfeudation and devolution of the de Burgo lordship and the 'King's Cantreds'. See also **256**.

258 LYDON (James Francis Michael). Edward II and the revenues of Ireland in 1311-12. In *I.H.S.*, xiv (1964-5), 39-57. (Select Documents, xxiv)

Introduction (pp 39-49) discusses the background of fiscal reform in England and financial embarrassment in Ireland.

259 LYDON (James Francis Michael). An Irish army in Scotland, 1296. In *Ir. Sword*, v (1961-2), 184-90.

Description, with an analytical table, of the Irish contingent for Edward I's Scottish campaign, and a discussion of its effects, especially on Irish finances.

260 LYDON (James Francis Michael). Irish levies in the Scottish wars, 1296-1302. In *Ir. Sword*, v (1961-2), 207-17.

Similar to **259**, with tables for 1300 and 1301, and for the allocation of shipping.

261 MACINERNY (M. Humbert). David MacKelly, archbishop of Cashel. In *I.E.R.*, 5th ser., iii (1914), 368-94, 505-19; iv (1914), 123-41.

Biography of David Ó Ceallaigh.

262 MACINERNY (M. Humbert). Primate Reginald of Armagh. In *I.E.R.*, 5th ser., vi (1915), 30-49, 157-80.

Controversies over the appointment of the bishop of Meath and the financing of Henry III's crusade, c.1253-4. See also M. O'Halloran, **265**.

263 McNAMARA (Leo F.). An examination of the medieval Irish text 'Caithréim Thoirdhealbhaigh': the historical value of the 'Caithréim Thoirdhealbhaigh'. In *N. Munster Antiq. Jn.*, viii (1958-61), 182-92.

> An important reassessment. See also E. Curtis, **252**, and T. J. Westropp, **277, 278**.

264 O'HALLORAN (Michael). Patrick O'Scannell, O.P., archbishop of Armagh, 1261-70. In *I.E.R.*, 5th ser., xciv (1960), 154-63.

265 O'HALLORAN (Michael). Primate Reginald and Henry III. In *I.E.R.*, 5th ser., lxxviii (1952), 121-9.

> See also M. H. MacInerny, **262**.

266 Ó MURCHADHA (Diarmuid). The battle of Callann, A.D. 1261. In *Cork Hist. Soc. Jn.*, lxvi (1961), 105-15.

> Discusses its background and significance.

267 ORPEN (Goddard Henry). Richard de Burgh and the conquest of Connaught. In *Galway Arch. Soc. Jn.*, vii (1911-12), 129-47.

> A detailed narrative, 1215-36. Cf. M. J. Blake, **214**.

268 O'SULLIVAN (Mary Donovan). Italian merchant bankers and the collection of papal revenues in Ireland in the thirteenth century. In *Galway Arch. Soc. Jn.*, xxii (1946-7), 132-63.

> See **270**.

269 O'SULLIVAN (Mary Donovan). Italian merchant bankers and the collection of the customs in Ireland, 1275-1311. In *Med. studies presented to A. Gwynn* (1961), pp 168-85.

> See **270**.

270 O'SULLIVAN (Mary Donovan). Italian merchant bankers in Ireland in the thirteenth century: a study in the social and economic history of medieval Ireland. Pp [5], 162. Dublin: Allen Figgis, 1962.

> The only major work on medieval Irish economic history, based on a thorough examination of the available sources. Incorporates material in **268, 269, 271**, with sections on money and trade. Bibliography. Map and family tree of Irish Cistercian houses, by H. G. Leask.

271 O'SULLIVAN (Mary Donovan). Some Italian merchant bankers in Ireland in the later thirteenth century. In *R.S.A.I. Jn.*, lxxix (1949), 10-19.

> See **270**.

272 POWICKE (*Sir* Frederick Maurice). The thirteenth century, 1216-1307. Pp xiv, 829. Oxford: Clarendon P., 1953. (The Oxford History of England, iv); 2nd ed. 1962.
'Ireland and Scotland, 1217-1297' (pp 560-617) includes an account of the state of Ireland (pp 560-71). Short narrative bibliography (pp 755-6).

273 RICHARDSON (Henry Gerald). Magna Carta Hiberniae. In *I.H.S.*, iii (1942-3), 31-3. (Historical Revision, v)
A re-examination of the authenticity of the alleged charter of 1217. See also R. Dudley Edwards, **253**.

274 RICHARDSON (Henry Gerald) *and* SAYLES (George Osborne). Irish revenue, 1278-1384. *R.I.A. Proc.*, lxii (1961-2), C, no. 4 (1962), 87-100.
Important survey of financial history. Some conclusions are questioned by J. F. Lydon in *I.H.S.*, xiii (1962-3), 261-3.

275 STRAYER (Joseph Reese) *and* RUDISILL (George). Taxation and community in Wales and Ireland, 1272-1327. In *Speculum*, xxix (1954), 410-16.
Consent to taxation and the significance of 'communitas'. See J. B. Morrall in *I.H.S.*, ix (1954-5), 239-41; J. F. Lydon in *E.H.R.*, lxxx (1955), 256.

276 SUTTON (R. J.). Robert de Ufford: tige des seigneurs de Poswick à la croix engrelée. Pp 85. Olne: F. Pirotte, 1968.
Includes chapters on his career in Ireland, pp 31-4, 51-66.

277 WESTROPP (Thomas Johnson). The Normans in Thomond. In *R.S.A.I. Jn.*, xxi (1890-1), 284-93, 381-7, 462-72.
A detailed narrative of the struggle between the de Clares and the O'Briens, 1276-1318. See also **278**.

278 WESTROPP (Thomas Johnson). On the external evidences bearing on the historic character of the 'Wars of Torlough' by John, son of Rory MacGrath. In *R.I.A. Trans.*, xxxii (1902-4), C, pt 2 (1903), 133-98.
The standard account, illustrated by photographs of relevant surviving buildings, etc. See also E. Curtis, **252**, and L. F. McNamara, **263**.

(e) THE BRUCE INVASION

279 ARMSTRONG (Olive Gertrude). Edward Bruce's invasion of Ireland. Pp xvi, 179. London: John Murray, 1923.

A detailed discussion of the invasion and its aftermath, with a long introductory analysis of the social and political background; but it should be used with caution and in conjunction with, especially, J. F. Lydon, **281**. Bibliography; 2 maps.

280 HORE (Herbert Francis). The Bruces in Ireland. In *U.J.A.*, v (1857), 1-12, 128-36; vi (1858), 66-76.

A paraphrase of the contemporary account by John Barbour.

281 LYDON (James Francis Michael). The Bruce invasion of Ireland. In *Hist. Studies*, iv (1963), 111-25.

An important reassessment in the context of the Anglo-Scottish war. Considers the relations of the Bruces with Ireland (1306-15), the position of Richard de Burgh, the financial crisis and Irish resources, and the war at sea. For the Scottish background see G. W. S. Barrow, *Robert Bruce and the community of the realm of Scotland* (London: Eyre & Spottiswoode, 1965).

282 MACARDLE (P. L.). Coronation of Edward Bruce. In *Louth Arch. Soc. Jn.*, iv (1916-20), 367-9.

An investigation of sites in the Dundalk area for Bruce's election, coronation and consecration, and for his court at Northburgh in 1315.

283 MACDONNELL (Peter). How was Edward Bruce killed? In *Louth Arch. Soc. Jn.*, ii (1908-11), 415-6.

A critical vindication of traditional accounts.

284 MACIVOR (Dermot). The battle of Fochart, 1318, by Diarmuid Mac Iomhair. In *Ir. Sword*, viii (1967-8), 192-209.

A detailed account. Map.

285 SAYLES (George Osborne). The battle of Faughart. In *The Irish at war* (1964), pp 23-34.

A general discussion of the Bruce invasion. Broadcast by R.E. as a Thomas Davis lecture in 1955; no mention of subsequent revision for publication.

286 WOOD (Herbert). Letter from Domnal O'Neill to Fineen MacCarthy, 1317. In *R.I.A. Proc.*, xxxvii (1924-7), C, no. 7 (1926), 141-8.

Mainly commentary on a rare example of a letter from one Irish chief to another, concerned with their collaboration with Bruce and appeal for papal support.

(f) THE FOURTEENTH CENTURY, 1316-99

287 BETTS (Reginald Robert). Richard Fitzralph, archbishop of Armagh, and the doctrine of dominion. In *Essays in British and Irish history in honour of James Eadie Todd*, ed. H. A. Cronne, T. W. Moody and D. B. Quinn (London: Muller, 1949), pp 46-60.
Thesis based on false premise—see A. Gwynn in *I.H.S.*, vii (1950-1), 131-3.

288 BYRNE (Patrick F.). Witchcraft in Ireland. Pp 76. Cork: Mercier P., 1967.
Includes 'Dame Alice Kyteler (the 14th century)', pp 18-27.

289 CLARKE (Maude Violet). William of Windsor in Ireland, 1369-1376. In *R.I.A. Proc.*, xli (1932-3), C, no. 2 (1932), 55-130; repr. in her *Fourteenth century studies* (1937; repr. 1969), pp 146-241.
An analysis of the opposition to Windsor's administration and the reshaping of the Irish parliament, now corrected in some respects by H. G. Richardson and G. O. Sayles, **354**, **355**, and by J. F. Lydon, **348**.

290 CURTIS (Edmund). Notes on episcopal succession in Ireland under Richard II. In *R.S.A.I. Jn.*, lvi (1926), 82-7.
A commentary on documents recording episcopal submissions and securing royal approval of elections. Supplementary to **292**.

291 CURTIS (Edmund). The pardon of Henry Blake of Galway in 1395. In *Galway Arch. Soc. Jn.*, xvi (1934-5), 186-9.
Introduction describes the incident as part of Richard II's policy of conciliation.

292 CURTIS (Edmund). Richard II in Ireland, 1394-5, and submissions of the Irish chiefs. Pp vii, 248. Oxford: Clarendon P., 1927.
Historical introduction (pp 1-54), and appendix giving details of each chief. Map. See also **290**.

293 CURTIS (Edmund). The viceroyalty of Lionel, duke of Clarence, in Ireland, 1361-1367. In *R.S.A.I. Jn.*, xlvii (1917), 165-81; xlviii (1918), 65-73.
Pt 1 is a general discussion of Irish politics and society at the time.

294 GLEESON (Dermot Florence). A fourteenth-century Clare heresy trial. In *I.E.R.*, 5th ser., lxxxix (1958), 36-42.
Conviction of two Irishmen of Clann Culein, 1353.

295 GWYNN (Aubrey Osborn). Richard II and the chieftains of Thomond. In *N. Munster Antiq. Jn.*, vii (1954-7), no. 3 (1956), 1-8.
A critical reappraisal of the documentary evidence for the events of 1394-5.

296 GWYNN (Aubrey Osborn). Richard FitzRalph, archbishop of Armagh. In *Studies*, xxii (1933), 389-405, 591-607; xxiii (1934), 395-411; xxiv (1935), 25-42, 558-72; xxv (1936), 81-96.
Title varies: Pt ii as 'Richard FitzRalph at Avignon'; pt iv 'The Black Death in Ireland'; pt v as 'Archbishop FitzRalph and George of Hungary'. A thorough biographical account, based on the sermon-diary (cf.**297**) and other sources.

297 GWYNN (Aubrey Osborn). The sermon-diary of Richard FitzRalph, archbishop of Armagh. In *R.I.A. Proc.*, xliv (1937-8), C, no. 1 (1937), 1-57.
A detailed analysis of the diary as a source for his career. See also **287, 296, 298.**

298 HAMMERICH (Louis Leonor). The beginning of the strife between Richard FitzRalph and the mendicants. With an edition of his autobiographical prayer and his proposition Unusquisque. Pp 85. Kobenhavn: Levin & Munksgaard, 1938. (Det Kongelige Danske Videnskabernes Selskab. Historisk-filologiske Meddelelser, xxvi, 3)

299 HAND (Geoffrey Joseph). The dating of the early fourteenth-century ecclesiastical valuations of Ireland. In *Ir. Theol. Quart.*, xxiv (1957), 271-4.
A concise examination, revealing reduced valuations following the Bruce invasion, and shedding light on the economic effects of this event.

300 HAND (Geoffrey Joseph). The forgotten statutes of Kilkenny: a brief survey. In *Ir. Jurist*, new ser., i (1966), 299-312.
A valuable analysis and discussion.

301 LEFF (Gordon). Richard FitzRalph, commentator of the Sentences: a study in theological orthodoxy. Pp viii, 200. Manchester: Manchester U.P., 1963.
See also his 'Richard Fitzralph's "Commentary on the Sentences" ' in *John Rylands Lib. Bull.*, xlv (1963), 390-422.

302 LYDON (James Francis Michael). Richard II's expeditions to Ireland. In *R.S.A.I. Jn.*, xciii (1963), 135-49.
An examination of motives, organisation, and significance. See also E. Curtis, **292.**

303 McKISACK (May). The fourteenth century, 1307-1399. Pp xix, 598. Oxford: Clarendon P., 1959. (The Oxford History of England, v)
Includes important passages on Ireland. These are scattered through the text and are best located through the index. Short narrative bibliography (pp 563-4).

304 NICHOLSON (Ranald George). Ireland and the Scottish wars of independence. In *I.C.H.S. Bull.*, new ser., ix (1962-3), nos 96-97 (Summer-Autumn 1962), p 1.

The significance of English intervention in Scotland for the failure to re-establish authority in Ireland.

305 NICHOLSON (Ranald George). An Irish expedition to Scotland in 1335. In *I.H.S.*, xiii (1962-3), 197-211.

Considers the Irish contribution to Edward III's campaign in Scotland and its significance in the decline of English hegemony in Ireland. Appendix analyses the composition of the force.

306 NICHOLSON (Ranald George). A sequel to Edward Bruce's invasion of Ireland. In *Scot. Hist. Rev.*, xlii (1963), 30-40.

An examination of Robert Bruce's visits to Ulster in 1327 and 1328, his attempt to secure Irish support for an invasion of Wales, and his truce with Mandeville.

307 ORPEN (Goddard Henry). The earldom of Ulster. In *R.S.A.I. Jn.*, xliii (1913), 30-46, 133-43; xliv (1914), 51-66: xlv (1915), 123-42; 1 (1920), 167-77; li (1921), 68-76.

Pt 6 erroneously numbered 5.

A detailed analysis of William de Burgh's estates in Ulster and some outlying districts, based on the inquisitions of 1333. For his lands in Connacht, see H. T. Knox, **257**.

308 OTWAY-RUTHVEN (Annette Jocelyn). Ireland in the 1350s: Sir Thomas de Rokeby and his successors. In *R.S.A.I. Jn.*, xcvii (1967), 47-59.

The efforts of successive justiciars to maintain royal authority over the Gaelic areas, 1348-61.

309 OTWAY-RUTHVEN (Annette Jocelyn). The partition of the de Verdon lands in Ireland in 1332. In *R.I.A. Proc.*, lxvi (1967-8), C, no. 5 (1968), 401-55.

Introduction (pp 401-20) contains a detailed analysis. 2 maps; genealogical table; index.

310 SAYLES (George Osborne). The rebellious first earl of Desmond. In *Med. studies presented to A. Gwynn* (1961), pp 203-29.

An account of his career, *c.*1293-1355, incorporating newly discovered evidence which has since been published as 'The legal proceedings against the first earl of Desmond', ed. G. O. Sayles in *Anal. Hib.*, xxiii (1966), 1-47.

311 TUCK (Anthony). Anglo-Irish relations, 1382-1393. In *R.I.A. Proc.*, lxix (1970), C, no. 2, 15-31.

Discusses the interaction of political events in England and Ireland.

312 WATT (John Anthony). Negotiations between Edward II and John XXII concerning Ireland. In *I.H.S.*, x (1956-7), 1-20.
Describes a largely ineffectual attempt at ecclesiastical reform.

313 WATT (John Anthony). Pope John XXII, King Edward II and Ireland. In *I.C.H.S. Bull.*, new ser., v (1956), no. 74, pp 1-2.
A summary of the evidence of the Barberini MSS in the Vatican Library. See also **312**.

(g) THE FIFTEENTH CENTURY, 1400-95

314 BERNARD (John Henry). Richard Talbot, archbishop and chancellor, 1418-1449. In *R.I.A. Proc.*, xxxv (1918-20), C, no. 5 (1919), 218-29.
A short biography.

315 BRYAN (Donough). Gerald FitzGerald, the Great Earl of Kildare, 1456-1513. Pp xxiii, 305. Dublin, Cork: Talbot P., 1933.
Published posthumously, with a foreword by E. Curtis. A predominantly reliable biography, containing much incidental information on constitutional issues. But heavily influenced by Curtis and M. V. Clarke, with old-fashioned views on 'constitutionalism'. See M. V. Clarke in *E.H.R.*, l (1935), 169.

316 BUTLER (George). The battle of Piltown, 1462. In *Ir. Sword*, vi (1963-4), 196-212.
Considered in the context of the Ormond-Desmond feud and the Wars of the Roses. Map.

317 BUTLER (Theobald Blake). Thomas le Botiller, prior of Kilmainham, 1403-1419. In *Ir. Geneal.*, ii (1943-55), 362-72.
Deputy, 1409-13, and leader of the Irish contingent in Henry V's French campaign, 1417-19.

318 CONWAY (Agnes). Henry VII's relations with Scotland and Ireland, 1485-1498. With a chapter on the acts of the Poynings' parliament, 1494-95, by Edmund Curtis. Pp xxxi, 260. Cambridge: Cambridge U.P., 1932.
Includes a detailed examination of Henry's policy in Ireland. Bibliography. See also **344**.

319 CURTIS (Edmund). Janico Dartas, Richard the Second's 'Gascon squire': his career in Ireland, 1394-1426. In *R.S.A.I. Jn.*, lxiii (1933), 182-205.

320 CURTIS (Edmund). Richard, duke of York, as viceroy of Ireland, 1447-1460; with unpublished materials for his relations with native chiefs. In *R.S.A.I. Jn.*, lxii (1932), 158-86.

321 GRIFFITH (Margaret Catherine). The Talbot-Ormond struggle for control of the Anglo-Irish government, 1414-47. In *I.H.S.*, ii (1940-1), 376-97.
A history of the feud, with a list of sources.

322 GWYNN (Aubrey Osborn). Canterbury and Armagh, 1414-1443. In *Studies*, xxxii (1943), 495-509.
Review of *The register of Henry Chichele, archbishop of Canterbury, 1414-1443*, ed. E. F. Jacob, vol. i (Oxford: Clarendon P., 1943; *also published as* Canterbury and York Series, xlv) in comparison with *The register of John Swayne, archbishop of Armagh and primate of Ireland, 1418-1439*, ed. D. A. Chart (Belfast: H.M.S.O., 1935. Northern Ireland Record Publication).

323 JACOB (Ernest Fraser). The fifteenth century, 1399-1485. Pp xvii, 775. Oxford: Clarendon P., 1961. (The Oxford History of England, vi)
The scattered references to Ireland should be read with caution. Short bibliography (p 721) contains serious errors.

324 MITCHELL (Rosamund Joscelyne). John Tiptoft, 1427-1470. Pp ix, 263. London, New York, Toronto: Longmans, Green, 1938.
'Tiptoft in Ireland' (pp 112-25) is a predominantly reliable account, despite the author's unfamiliarity with the Irish sources and background. See D. B. Quinn in *I.H.S.*, iii (1942-3), 335-8.

325 QUINN (David Beers). The Irish parliamentary subsidy in the fifteenth and sixteenth centuries. In *R.I.A. Proc.*, xlii (1934-5), C, no. 11 (1935), 219-46.
An examination of the system and its application. For its origins, see M. V. Clarke, **289**, pp 66-74.

VI MILITARY HISTORY

See also **231, 259, 260, 266, 284, 285, 305, 316.**

326 DUGGAN (G. C.). Troop movements in the Irish Sea. In *Ir. Sword*, ix (1969-70), 174-82.

Includes discussion of the importance of sea communications in the middle ages, especially under Edward I.

327 HAYES-MCCOY (Gerard Anthony). The early history of guns in Ireland. In *Galway Arch. Soc. Jn.*, xviii (1938-9), 43-65.

Includes a chronological study of contemporary references to firearms, 1487-1513.

328 HAYES-MCCOY (Gerard Anthony). The gallóglach axe. In *Galway Arch. Soc. Jn.*, xvii (1936-7), 101-21.

A detailed account, based mainly on 16th-century evidence, but drawing on earlier sources for its use. See also the note by Adolf Mahr on two recent acquisitions by N.M.I. in *Galway Arch. Soc. Jn.*, xviii (1938-9), 66-7; and Professor Hayes-McCoy's reply, *ibid.*, pp 67-8.

329 HAYES-MCCOY (Gerard Anthony), *ed.* The Irish at war. Pp 108. Cork: Mercier P., 1964.

Thomas Davis lectures, broadcast by R.E., 1955-6. See G. O. Sayles, **285.**

330 HAYES-MCCOY (Gerard Anthony). Irish battles. Pp viii, 326. London: Longmans, 1969.

A pioneer military history of Ireland, concentrating on detailed descriptions of 14 individual battles, including Dublin, 1171, and Dysert O'Dea, 1318 (pp 22-47). Maps and plates; but references confined to short reading lists of the more accessible material. See J. G. Simms in *I.H.S.*, xvi (1968-9), 499-501.

331 HAYES-MCCOY (Gerard Anthony). Scots mercenary forces in Ireland, 1565-1603: an account of their service during that period, of the reaction of their activities on Scottish affairs, and of the effect of their presence in Ireland; together with an examination of the gallóglaigh or galloglas. With an introduction by Eoin MacNeill. Pp xxi, 391. Dublin, London: Burns, Oates & Washbourne, 1937.

'The gallóglaigh' (pp 15-76) is a thorough study, including the medieval period.

332 HAYES-MCCOY (Gerard Anthony). Strategy and tactics in later medieval Ireland: a general survey. In *I.C.H.S. Bull.*, no. 20 (May 1942), 1-3.

12th-15th centuries.

333 LYDON (James Francis Michael). The hobelar: an Irish contribution to mediaeval warfare. In *Ir. Sword*, ii (1954-6), 12-16.
A concise description and history of the Irish light horseman.

334 McKERRAL (Andrew). West Highland mercenaries in Ireland. In *Scot. Hist. Rev.*, xxx (1951), 1-14.
An examination of the origins and nature of the galloglasses and their contribution to the Gaelic resistance movement, *c.*1290-1602.

335 MacNEILL (Eoin). Military service in medieval Ireland. In *Cork Hist. Soc. Jn.*, xlvi (1941), 6-15.
The organisation of native Irish forces in pre-Elizabethan times.

336 Ó BÁILLE (M.). The buannadha: Irish professional soldiery of the sixteenth century. In *Galway Arch. Soc. Jn.*, xxii (1946-7), 49-94.
Includes a refutation of the existence of this type of Irish mercenary in the middle ages.

337 O'CONNELL (Jeremiah J.). Kern and galloglas. With illustrations drawn from contemporary documents by Séamus MacCall. In *An Cosantóir: a monthly review for all branches of the defence forces* (Dublin: Department of Defence), iii (1943), 151-3, 267-71.
Detailed description of dress, arms and organisation, relating mainly to the 16th century. Sources not specified.

338 O'CONNOR (Patrick). Hurdle making in Dublin, 1302-3. In *Dublin Hist. Rec.*, xiii (1952-4), 18-22.
Includes commentary on an account of William de Moenes for making hurdles for the army in Scotland.

339 OTWAY-RUTHVEN (Annette Jocelyn). Knight service in Ireland. In *R.S.A.I. Jn.*, lxxxix (1959), 1-15.
An authoritative examination of military feudalism, including a discussion of the standard fee.

340 OTWAY-RUTHVEN (Annette Jocelyn). Royal service in Ireland. In *R.S.A.I. Jn.*, xcviii (1968), 37-46.
Chronological, annotated list of scutages, prefaced by a historical discussion.

VII CONSTITUTIONAL AND ADMINISTRATIVE HISTORY

(a) COUNCIL AND PARLIAMENT

See also **275, 289, 325.**

341 ARMSTRONG (Olive Gertrude). Manuscripts of the 'Modus tenendi parliamentum' in the Library of Trinity College, Dublin. In *R.I.A. Proc.*, xxxvi (1921-4), C, no. 15 (1923), 256-64.
See note on **343** below.

342 CLARKE (Maude Violet). Irish parliaments in the reign of Edward II. In *R. Hist. Soc. Trans.*, 4th ser., ix (1926), 29-62; repr. in her *Fourteenth century studies* (1937; repr. 1969), pp 1-35.
A consideration of the persistent efforts to solve the problems of Irish disorder by parliamentary means; now requiring revision in some respects in the light of more recent research. Appendices list Irish parliaments (1309-27), subtenants summoned in 1310, bishoprics vacant, and sources of Irish revenue.

343 CLARKE (Maude Violet). Medieval representation and consent: a study of early parliaments in England and Ireland, with special reference to the Modus tenendi parliamentum. Pp vii, 408. London, New York, Toronto: Longmans, Green, 1936.
Includes chapters on 'The Irish church and taxation in the later middle ages' (pp 33-69); 'The manuscripts of the Irish Modus' (pp 70-95); 'The Irish Modus: its history' (pp 96-124). See also Olive Armstrong, **341**; H. M. Cam in *E.H.R.*, li (1936), 701-4; V. H. Galbraith, 'The Modus tenendi parliamentum' in *Journal of the Warburg and Courtauld Institutes*, xvi (1953), 81-99, which discusses the Irish 'Modus' in an appendix, 'The priority of the English Modus' (pp 95-9); H. G. Richardson, **352**, and in *History*, new ser., xxii (1937-8), 66-9; and John Taylor, 'The manuscripts of the Modus tenendi parliamentum' in *E.H.R.*, lxxxiii (1968), 673-88, where the footnotes provide an up-to-date bibliography of the subject.

344 CURTIS (Edmund). The acts of the Drogheda parliament, 1494-5, or 'Poynings' laws'. In *Henry VII's relations with Scotland and Ireland, 1485-1498*, by Agnes Conway (1932), pp 118-43.
A summary of the legislation, with a discussion of its purpose and significance. See also R. Dudley Edwards and T. W. Moody, **345**, and D. B. Quinn, **350**.

345 EDWARDS (Robert Walter Dudley) *and* MOODY (Theodore William). The history of Poynings' law. Part i. 1494-1615. In *I.H.S.*, ii (1940-1), 145-24. (Historical Revision, iv)
Includes a reassessment of the operation of the act during the pre-Reformation period, 1494-1534. See also E. Curtis, **344**, and D. B. Quinn, **350**.

346 JOHNSTON (William John). The English legislature and the Irish courts. In *Law Quart. Rev.*, xl (1924), 91-106.

Concerned mainly with the constitutional position of the Irish parliament and the status of English legislation in medieval Ireland.

347 LYDON (James Francis Michael). The Irish church and taxation in the fourteenth century. In *I.E.R.*, 5th ser., ciii (1965), 158-65; repr. in *Ir. Cath. Hist. Comm. Proc.*, 1964, pp 3-10.

An examination of the system of consent to clerical subsidies and of the powers of proctors in the Irish parliament or great council.

348 LYDON (James Francis Michael). William of Windsor and the Irish parliament. In *E.H.R.*, lxxx (1965), 252-67.

A re-examination of Windsor's quarrel with the Irish commons, 1369-76, and its bearing on the powers of representatives. See also M. V. Clarke, **289.**

349 O'HANLON (John). Irish parliaments. In *I.E.R.*, 3rd ser., xii (1891), 116-33, 212-24.

A short history from origins to Union. No longer a reliable guide to the medieval period.

350 QUINN (David Beers). The early interpretation of Poynings' law, 1494-1534. In *I.H.S.*, ii (1940-1), 241-54.

A discussion of its operation. See also corrections by the author in *I.H.S.*, iii (1942-3), 106-7; E. Curtis, **344**; R. D. Edwards and T. W. Moody, **345.**

351 QUINN (David Beers). Parliaments and great councils in Ireland, 1461-1586. In *I.H.S.*, iii (1942-3), 60-77.

A report on behalf of the Assemblies-of-estates sub-committee of I.C.H.S. Chronological table listing place and date of meetings, prorogations, etc., and king's representatives.

352 RICHARDSON (Henry Gerald). The Preston exemplification of the Modus tenendi parliamentum. In *I.H.S.*, iii (1942-3), 187-92. (Historical Revision, vii)

A reassessment of the authenticity of the document in the possession of Sir Christopher Preston in 1419. Criticises views expressed by M. V. Clarke, **343**, and A. Gwynn in *Studies*, xxxi (1942), 47-64. See also J. Otway-Ruthven in *I.H.S.*, xvi (1968-9), 212-3.

353 RICHARDSON (Henry Gerald) *and* SAYLES (George Osborne). The Irish parliaments of Edward I. In *R.I.A. Proc.*, xxxviii (1928-9), C, no. 6 (1929), 128-47.

An outline history.

354 RICHARDSON (Henry Gerald) *and* SAYLES (George Osborne). The Irish parliament in the middle ages. Pp x, 395. Philadelphia: Univ. of Pennsylvania P.; London: Oxford U.P., 1952. (Etudes présentées à la Commission Internationale pour l'Histoire des Assemblées d'Etats, x); 2nd ed. 1964.
> Definitive study, with comprehensive bibliography and indexes. 2nd ed. is merely a reprint with minor corrections. For corrections and additions to the chronological list of parliaments and councils, 1264-1495 (pp 332-65) see J. Otway-Ruthven in *I.H.S.*, xvi (1968-9), 214. For earlier criticism see A. Gwynn, 'The Irish parliament in the middle ages' in *Studies*, xlii (1953), 209-22; and C. H. McIlwain in *I.H.S.*, ix (1954-5), 86-8.

355 RICHARDSON (Henry Gerald) *and* SAYLES (George Osborne). Parliament in medieval Ireland. Pp 28. Dundalk: Dundalgan P., for Dublin Historical Association, 1964. (Medieval Irish History Series, no. 1)
> A useful epitome of **354.**

356 WATT (John Anthony). The first recorded use of the word 'parliament' in Ireland? In *Ir. Jur.*, new ser., iv (1969), 123-6.
> The abbreviation 'parle' in a summary transcript of the Irish pipe roll for 1235.

(b) ADMINISTRATIVE AND JUDICIAL INSTITUTIONS

Although much has been published on individual institutions, there is no comprehensive work on Irish constitutional or administrative history. The best short survey is in A. J. Otway-Ruthven, **211**, pp 144-90.

357 HUGHES (James L. J.). Patentee officers in Ireland, 1173-1826, including high sheriffs, 1661-1684 and 1761-1816. Pp vii, 142. Dublin: Stationery Office, 1960. (I.M.C.)

An alphabetical list of office-holders in the destroyed Irish patent rolls as recorded in Rowley Lascelles, *Liber munerum publicorum Hiberniae ab an. 1152 usque ad 1827; or, The establishments of Ireland* . . . (2 vols, London, 1824-30, i.e. 1852), and the Lodge MSS in P.R.O.I.

358 RICHARDSON (Henry Gerald) *and* SAYLES (George Osborne). The administration of Ireland, 1172-1377. Pp xiii, 300. Dublin: Stationery Office, 1963. (I.M.C.)

Lists of ministers, judges, and Irish treasurers' accounts, with an introduction (pp 1-69) describing the central administrative system and offices; local government is not covered.

(c) CENTRAL GOVERNMENT

(i) Chief Governor

359 OTWAY-RUTHVEN (Annette Jocelyn). The chief governors of mediaeval Ireland. In *R.S.A.I. Jn.*, xcv (1965), 227-36.

A comprehensive survey and analysis of the office, function and powers from 12th to 15th centuries.

360 WOOD (Herbert). The office of chief governor of Ireland, 1172-1509. In *R.I.A. Proc.*, xxxvi (1921-4), C, no. 12 (1923), 206-38.

A discussion of titles and functions, with a chronological list, since corrected by that in *Handbook of British chronology*, ed. F. M. Powicke and E. B. Fryde, 2nd ed. (London: Royal Historical Society, 1961. Guides and Handbooks, no. 2), pp 147-68.

361 WOOD (Herbert). The titles of the chief governors of Ireland. In *I.H.R. Bull.*, xiii (1935-6), 1-8.

An explanation of the varying titles.

362 WOOD (Herbert). Two chief governors of Ireland at the same time. In *R.S.A.I. Jn.*, lviii (1928), 156-7.

A short note on the period 12 May 1453-3/15 April 1454, when Richard, duke of York, and James, earl of Ormond both claimed office during the former's disgrace.

(ii) Chancery

363 OTWAY-RUTHVEN (Annette Jocelyn). The mediaeval Irish chancery. In *Album Helen Maud Cam*, ii (Louvain: Publications universitaires de Louvain; Paris: Nauwelaerts, 1961. Etudes présentées à la Commission Internationale pour l'Histoire des Assemblées d'Etats, xxiv), pp 119-38.

An outline of the development of the institution and the remuneration of its officers, 1232-*c*.1485. Lists of chancellors (including deputies and keepers of the great seal), keepers of the rolls of chancery, clerks of the hanaper, and clerks of the crown in chancery, 1377-1485. For officials prior to 1377 see H. G. Richardson and G. O. Sayles, **358**; for brief biographies of chancellors and keepers of the rolls see F. E. Ball, **367**.

(iii) Exchequer

There is no comprehensive account of the Irish exchequer, but the items listed in this section collectively shed some light on it. There is also a brief description in A. J. Otway-Ruthven, **211**, pp 152-3.

364 DAVIES (Oliver) *and* QUINN (David Beers), *ed.* The Irish pipe roll of 14 John, 1211-1212. Pp 73. Belfast: Ulster Archaeological Society, 1941. (*U.J.A.*, 3rd ser., iv, supplement)

Introduction (pp 1-6) includes a brief account of the Irish exchequer. See also H. G. Richardson, **236**, and *U.J.A.*, *Index and corrigenda, 3rd ser.*, *i-vi*, pp 27-36.

365 LYDON (James Francis Michael). The Irish exchequer in the thirteenth century. In *I.C.H.S. Bull.*, new ser., vi (1957-8), no. 81 (Feb. 1958), 1-2.

A short account of its development.

366 LYDON (James Francis Michael). Three exchequer documents from the reign of Henry the Third. In *R.I.A. Proc.*, lxv (1966-7), C, no. 1 (1966), 1-27.

Introduction (pp 1-18) contains much information on the workings of the exchequer.

(iv) Judiciary

367 BALL (Francis Elrington). The judges in Ireland, 1221-1921. 2 vols. London: John Murray, 1926; New York: Dutton, 1927.

Historical narrative, succession to judicial offices, and a biographical catalogue of their holders. For more complete lists of some officers see J. Otway-Ruthven, **363**, and H. G. Richardson and G. O. Sayles, **358**.

368 HAND (Geoffrey Joseph). The common law in Ireland in the thirteenth and fourteenth centuries: two cases involving Christ Church, Dublin. In *R.S.A.I. Jn.*, xcvii (1967), 97-111.

Complex examples of wardship and regalian right, illustrating the repercussions of the application of English law in Ireland.

369 HAND (Geoffrey Joseph). English law in Ireland, 1290-1324. Pp xi, 280. Cambridge: Cambridge U.P., 1967. (Cambridge Studies in English Legal History)

A thorough analysis of the Irish judiciary. Appendices include a list of justices itinerant, 1248-69, lists and analyses of justiciary rolls and rolls of the Dublin Bench, list of itinerant justices' rolls. Bibliography; table of statutes. See J. F. Lydon in *E.H.R.*, lxxxv (1970), 156-7.

370 HAND (Geoffrey Joseph). Procedure without writ in the court of the justiciar of Ireland. In *R.I.A. Proc.*, lxii (1961-3), C, no. 2 (1961), 9-20.

Considers the categories of action without writ, the effect of the itinerant nature of the court, reasons for its popularity, and contemporary criticism of it.

371 JOHNSTON (William John). Ireland in the medieval law courts. In *Studies*, xii (1923), 553-70.

A discussion of miscellaneous cases.

(d) LOCAL GOVERNMENT

372 ALTSCHUL (Michael). A baronial family in medieval England: the Clares, 1217-1314. Pp 332. Baltimore: Johns Hopkins P., 1965. (The Johns Hopkins University Studies in Historical and Political Science, ser. 83, no. 2)

'Lord of Kilkenny' (pp 281-95) contains a useful account of the administration of the liberty of Kilkenny; printed sources are occasionally misinterpreted.

373 BERRY (Henry Fitzpatrick). Sheriffs of the county Cork: Henry III to 1660. In *R.S.A.I. Jn.*, xxxv (1905), 39-48.

Introduction and chronological list.

374 BUTLER (Theobald Blake). Seneschals of the liberty of Tipperary. In *Ir. Geneal.*, ii (1943-55), 294-302, 326-36, 368-76; iii (1956-67), 46-59, 109-15.

A calendar of documentary references to each seneschal, 1328-1705, arranged chronologically, with a list of grants, forfeitures, etc., affecting the liberty.

375 DELANY (Vincent Thomas Hyginas). The palatinate court of the liberty of Tipperary. In *Amer. Jn. Legal Hist.*, v (1961), 95-117.

A survey to 1715. The medieval section should be read with caution.

376 DOLLEY (Reginald Hugh Michael). The first treasure trove inquest in Ireland? In *N.I. Legal Quart.*, xix (1967-8), 182-8.

Examines the evidence for a possible coin-find in 1215.

377 FRAME (Robert Ferris). The judicial powers of the medieval Irish keepers of the peace. In *Ir. Jurist*, new ser., ii (1967), 308-26.

A thorough study of the evolution of the offices of keeper and justice of the peace, in comparison with their English counterparts.

378 McNEILL (Charles). The secular jurisdiction of the early archbishops of Dublin. In *R.S.A.I. Jn.*, xlv (1915), 81-108.

Introduction (pp 81-8) examines the evidence of Alen's Register for the temporal jurisdiction of the manorial courts of the archbishopric. The extracts printed here have since been calendared more fully in *Calendar of Archbishop Alen's Register, c.1172-1534,* ed. C. McNeill (Dublin: R.S.A.I., 1950. Extra vol., 1949).

379 MEGHEN (P. J.). The development of Irish local government. In *Administration* (Dublin: Institute of Public Administration), viii (1960), 333-46.

Concerned mainly with 18th century and later, but includes a very brief survey of medieval development.

380 MILLS (James). Accounts of the earl of Norfolk's estates in Ireland, 1279-1294. In *R.S.A.I. Jn.*, xxii (1892), 50-62.

Describes the administration of Roger Bigod's lordship of Carlow, 1270-1306, as revealed by account rolls in P.R.O. See also W. F. Nugent, **381.**

381 NUGENT (William Francis). Carlow in the middle ages. In *R.S.A.I. Jn.*, lxxxv (1955), 62-76.

A detailed account of the liberty and its administration in the 13th century. See also J. Mills, **380.**

382 OTWAY-RUTHVEN (Annette Jocelyn). Anglo-Irish local government in the late thirteenth century. In *I.C.H.S. Bull.*, no. 41 (December 1945), 1-3.

Superseded by **383.**

383 OTWAY-RUTHVEN (Annette Jocelyn). Anglo-Irish shire government in the thirteenth century. In *I.H.S.*, v (1946-7), 1-28.

Traces the introduction of the shire system to Ireland and discusses its organisation, relations with the great liberties and crosslands, and the functions of the sheriff and his subordinates. See also **384.**

384 OTWAY-RUTHVEN (Annette Jocelyn). The medieval county of Kildare. In *I.H.S.*, xi (1958-9), 181-99.

A detailed analysis of the territorial structure and constitution of the liberty before 1345. Map.

385 QUINN (David Beers). Anglo-Irish local government, 1485-1534. In *I.H.S.*, i (1938-9), 354-81.

A general description.

386 WOOD (Herbert). The muniments of Edmund de Mortimer, third earl of March, concerning his liberty of Trim. In *R.I.A. Proc.*, xl (1931-2), C, no. 7 (1932), 312-55.

Includes (pp 312-19) an account of the history and constitutional position of the liberty.

VIII ECCLESIASTICAL HISTORY

(a) GENERAL

387   DUNNING (Patrick Joseph). The letters of Innocent III as a source for Irish history. In *Ir. Cath. Hist. Comm. Proc.*, 1958, pp 1-10.
Describes the various types of papal letter in detail and discusses their limitations as source material.

388   FLANAGAN (Urban Gerard). The church in Ireland in the mid-fifteenth century. In *I.C.H.S. Bull.*, new ser., i, no. 62 (Sept. 1952), 6-7.
A survey of the sources and the problems of their interpretation.

389   GWYNN (Aubrey Osborn). Ireland and the English nation at the Council of Constance. In *R.I.A. Proc.*, xlv (1938-40), C, no. 8 (1940), 183-233.
Valuable for Irish ecclesiastical affairs and attitudes during the Schism, and for the early career of John Swayne.

390   GWYNN (Aubrey Osborn). The medieval province of Armagh, 1470-1545. Pp xi, 287. Dundalk: W. Tempest, Dundalgan P., 1946.
A very detailed commentary on the Armagh registers, yielding a valuable picture of diocesan life. Discusses individual archbishops and bishops, and describes the diocesan organisation. Short bibliography.

391   GWYNN (Aubrey Osborn) *and* GLEESON (Dermot Florence). A history of the diocese of Killaloe. [Vol. i.] Pp xvii, 566. Dublin: Gill, [1962].
Professor Gwynn's chapter 'The origins of the diocese of Killaloe' (pp 90-131) contains an excellent account of the 12th-century reform movement in Ireland. It is complementary to his *The twelfth century reform* (see **392**), and summarises a number of his earlier articles; these are listed in *Med. studies presented to A. Gwynn*, pp 502-7. The late Dr Gleeson's section unfortunately contains many inaccuracies and must be used with great caution—see J. F. Lydon in *I.H.S.*, xiv (1964-5), 67-70.

392   A HISTORY OF IRISH CATHOLICISM. General editor: Patrick J. Corish. Dublin, Melbourne, etc.: Gill, 1967-   .
Vol. ii. The later medieval church.
    1. Aubrey Gwynn, *The twelfth century reform*. Pp 68. 1968.
    3. Geoffrey Hand, *The church in the English lordship, 1216-1307*. Pp 43. 1968.
    4. Aubrey Gwynn, *Anglo-Irish church life: fourteenth and fifteenth centuries*. Pp 76. 1968.
    5. Canice Mooney, *The church in Gaelic Ireland*. Pp 62. 1970.
Vol. ii, fascs 3-4 published in one part. The work as a whole will be completed in 6 vols, covering the period from St Patrick to 20th century. Imprint varies: Dublin: Gill & Macmillan, 1970-   .

393 Lucas (Anthony Thomas). The plundering and burning of churches in Ireland, 7th to 16th century. In *North Munster studies* (1967), pp 172-229.

All recorded instances listed alphabetically by church or monastery (pp 215-23), with a chronological list of collective attacks (pp 223-8). The article itself includes an important discussion of sanctuary, especially with regard to lay property.

394 Mooney (Canice). Ciníochas agus náisiúnachas san eaglais in Éirinn, 1169-1534, [by] Cainneach Ó Maonaigh. In *Galvia*, x (1964-5), 4-17.

Three lectures delivered under the auspices of An Oireachtas, originally published as 'Racialism and nationalism in the Irish church' in *Innui*, 25 Oct., 1 and 8 Nov., 1963. Both versions in Irish.

395 Ó Briain (Felim). The expansion of Irish christianity to 1200: an historiographical survey. In *I.H.S.*, iii (1942-3), 241-66; iv (1944-5), 131-63.

A discussion of sources and techniques for research on the influence of Irish christianity on the continent.

396 Otway-Ruthven (Annette Jocelyn). The mediaeval church lands of Co. Dublin. In *Med. studies presented to A. Gwynn* (1961), pp 54-73.

Analyses and identifies the crosslands of the county. Map at end of vol.

397 Phillips (Walter Alison), *ed.* History of the Church of Ireland from the earliest times to the present day. 3 vols. London: Oxford U.P., 1933.

Vol. ii includes chapters by G. H. Orpen, 'Anglo-Norman influence' (pp 50-77) and St J. D. Seymour, 'The medieval church, 1216-1509' (pp 78-168). Bibliography.

398 Ronan (Myles Vincent). Anglo-Norman Dublin and diocese. In *I.E.R.*, 5th ser., xlv (1935), 148-64, 274-91, 485-504, 576-95; xlvi (1935), 11-30, 154-71, 257-75, 377-93, 490-510, 577-96; xlvii (1936), 28-44, 144-63, 459-68; xlviii (1936), 170-93, 378-96; xlix (1937), 155-64.

Primarily a history of church and state in the diocese from the 12th century to 1509, but of more than local significance.

399 Ronan (Myles Vincent). Religious customs of Dublin medieval gilds. In *I.E.R.*, 5th ser., xxvi (1925), 224-47, 364-85.

Deals with both trade and socio-religious gilds.

400 STOKES (George Thomas). Ireland and the Anglo-Norman church: a history of Ireland and Irish christianity from the Anglo-Norman conquest to the dawn of the Reformation. Pp xvi, 391. London: Hodder & Stoughton, 1889.
Superseded in many respects by *A history of Irish catholicism*, **292**, and W. Alison Phillips, **297**.

401 WATT (John Anthony). The church and the two nations in medieval Ireland. Pp xvi, 251. Cambridge: Cambridge U.P., 1970 (Cambridge Studies in Medieval Life and Thought, 3rd ser., vol. 3)
5 maps.

(b) GOVERNMENT AND ORGANISATION

402 BARRY (John Gerard). The coarb and the twelfth-century reform. In *I.E.R.*, 5th ser., lxxxviii (1957), 17-25.—The coarb in medieval times. In *I.E.R.*, 5th ser., lxxxix (1958), 24-35.—The erenagh in the monastic Irish church. In *I.E.R.*, 5th ser., lxxxix (1958), 424-32. —The lay coarb in medieval times. In *I.E.R.*, 5th ser., xci (1959), 27-39.—The appointment of coarb and erenagh. In *I.E.R.*, 5th ser., xciii (1960), 361-5.—The extent of coarb and erenagh in Gaelic Ulster. In *I.E.R.*, 5th ser., xciv (1960), 12-16.—The distinction between coarb and erenagh. In *I.E.R.*, 5th ser., xciv (1960), 90-5.—The status of coarbs and erenaghs. In *I.E.R.*, 5th ser., (1960), 147-53.—The duties of coarbs and erenaghs. In *I.E.R.*, 5th ser., xciv (1960), 211-18.

> Together these articles provide a comprehensive study of the medieval coarb and erenagh.

403 BRADY (John). Anglo-Norman organization of the diocese of Meath. In *I.E.R.*, 5th ser., lxvii (1946), 232-7.

> Demonstrates the effects of reform and invasion on diocesan organisation.

404 BRADY (John). The cathedral and chapter of Meath. In *I.E.R.*, 5th ser., lii (1938), 286-92; liv (1939), 269-76.

405 CHENEY (Christopher Robert). A group of related synodal statutes of the thirteenth century. In *Med. studies presented to A. Gwynn* (1961), pp 114-32.

> A thorough enquiry into the origin and relationship of three sets of diocesan statutes—of Dublin, Chichester and York—demonstrating their interdependence and shedding light on methods of diocesan legislating in Ireland.

406 GWYNN (Aubrey Osborn). The diocese of Limerick in the twelfth century. In *N. Munster Antiq. Jn.*, v (1946-8), 35-48.

> A study of changes in Limerick in the context of diocesan reorganisation in Ireland as a whole.

407 HAND (Geoffrey Joseph). The church and English law in medieval Ireland. In *Ir. Cath. Hist. Comm. Proc.*, 1959, pp 10-18.

> Examines the questions of ecclesiastical property and privilege, advowsons, and ecclesiastical jurisdiction affecting secular courts.

408 HAND (Geoffrey Joseph). Mediaeval cathedral chapters. In *Ir. Cath. Hist. Comm. Proc.*, 1956, pp 11-14.

> A short survey of the types of chapter organisation in medieval Ireland, and the sources for their study. See also **409**.

409 HAND (Geoffrey Joseph). The medieval chapter of St Patrick's Cathedral, Dublin. 1. The early period, c.1219-c.1279. In *Reportorium Novum*, iii (1961-4), 229-48.
A detailed account of its organisation.

410 HAND (Geoffrey Joseph). The rivalry of the cathedral chapters in medieval Dublin. In *R.S.A.I. Jn.*, xcii (1962), 193-206.
A historical account, demonstrating the persistent, underlying conflict between Celtic and Anglo-Norman traditions.

411 IRISH CATHOLIC HISTORICAL COMMITTEE. CONFERENCE ON DIOCESAN AND LOCAL HISTORY, Easter 1956. The church in the fifteenth century. In *Ir. Cath. Hist. Comm. Proc.*, 1956, pp 1-16.
Includes papers on diocesan organisation by J. O'Connell, Patrick K. Egan, Denis Buckley, with a summary by Patrick J. Corish. See also G. J. Hand, **408**.

412 MacENERNEY (F.). The origin and value of the distinction 'Primate of Ireland', 'Primate of All Ireland'. In *I.E.R.*, 3rd ser., x (1889), 422-32
A discussion of the origins and significance of the Armagh-Dublin controversy.

413 MASON (William Monck). The history and antiquities of the collegiate and cathedral church of St Patrick near Dublin, from its foundation in 1190 to the year 1819; comprising a topographical account of the lands and parishes appropriated to the community of the cathedral and to its members, and biographical memoirs of its deans. Pp [8], 479, xcvii. Dublin: printed for the author by W. Folds, 1820.
Still valuable as an accurate and scholarly work, in spite of its age. Illustrated.

414 NICHOLLS (Kenneth William). The episcopal rentals of Clonfert and Kilmacduagh. In *Anal. Hib.*, xxvi (1971), 130-43.
Introduction covering 13th-17th centuries (pp 130-35).

415 OTWAY-RUTHVEN (Annette Jocelyn). Parochial development in the rural deanery of Skreen. In *R.S.A.I. Jn.*, xciv (1964), 111-22.
Traces the origins and development of parochial organisation in Norman Ireland, c.1172-1622, with a detailed analysis of Skreen. 2 maps.

416 SAYLES (George Osborne). Ecclesiastical process and the parsonage of Stabannon in 1351: a study of the medieval Irish church in action. In *R.I.A. Proc.*, lv (1952-3), C, no. 1 (1952), 1-23.
An absorbing picture of the machinery of church government, revealed through a detailed account of an individual case.

417 SAYLES (George Osborne). Who was the parson of Stabannon in 1351? In *I.C.H.S. Bull.*, no. 57 (April 1948), 5-6.
A brief preliminary summary of **416**.

418 SEYMOUR (St John Drelincourt). The coarb in the medieval Irish church, *circa* 1200-1550. In *R.I.A. Proc.*, xli (1932-4), C, no. 10 (1933), 219-31.
A careful examination of the nature of the office and its holders. See also J. G. Barry, **402**.

419 WATT (John Anthony). English law and the Irish church: the reign of Edward I. In *Med. studies presented to A. Gwynn* (1961), pp 133-67.
An important analysis of church-state relations, especially over the questions of episcopal elections, custody of temporalities, the clergy and the common law, and the respective jurisdictions of ecclesiastical and temporal courts. See also G. J. Hand, **407**.

(c) RELATIONS WITH THE PAPACY

420 DUNNING (Patrick Joseph). Irish representatives and Irish ecclesiastical affairs at the Fourth Lateran Council. In *Med. studies presented to A. Gwynn* (1961), pp 90-113.

An examination of the evidence and the light it sheds on Irish ecclesiastical affairs.

421 DUNNING (Patrick Joseph). Pope Innocent III and the Ross election controversy. In *Ir. Theol. Quart.*, xxvi (1959), 346-59.

A study of the disputed election of 1198 and the difficulties of appealing to the Papacy.

422 DUNNING (Patrick Joseph). Pope Innocent III and the Waterford-Lismore controversy, 1198-1216. In *Ir. Theol. Quart.*, xxviii (1961), 215-32.

Irish canonical procedure illustrated by a detailed account of attempts by bishops of Waterford to absorb the see of Lismore.

423 EDWARDS (Robert Walter Dudley). Conflict of papal and royal jurisdictions in fifteenth century Ireland. In *Ir. Cath. Hist. Comm. Proc.*, 1960, pp 3-9.

An introductory survey; for a more detailed treatment see **424.**

424 EDWARDS (Robert Walter Dudley). The kings of England and papal provisions in fifteenth-century Ireland. In *Med. studies presented to A. Gwynn* (1961), pp 265-80.

Considers examples of conflicting jurisdictions in the context of royal endeavours to secure the election of loyal nominees.

425 FLANAGAN (Urban Gerard). Papal letters of the fifteenth century as a source for Irish history. In *Ir. Cath. Hist. Comm. Proc.*, 1958, pp 11-15.

An introduction to material important for the study of papal provisions

426 FLANAGAN (Urban Gerard). Papal provisions in Ireland, 1305-78. In *Hist. Studies*, iii (1961), 92-103.

A discussion of the theory and practice of the system, with a close examination of the papal attempt to influence Irish appointments during the 'Babylonish Captivity'.

427 WATT (John Anthony). The Papacy and episcopal appointments in thirteenth-century Ireland. In *Ir. Cath. Hist. Comm. Proc.*, 1959, pp 1-9.

An admirable survey of papal policy towards Ireland.

428 WILLIAMSON (Dorothy M.). The legate Otto in Scotland and Ireland, 1237-1240. In *Scot. Hist. Rev.*, xxviii (1949), 12-30.

Includes discussion of papal intervention in Irish elections, and the conflict between Anglo-Norman and Irish elements, Roman and Celtic observances, in the Irish church.

(d) RELIGIOUS ORDERS

(i) General

429 ALEMAND (Louis), Histoire monastique d'Irlande. Pp [4], 438. Paris: Louis Lucas, 1690; *English translation by John Stevens as* Monasticon Hibernicum; or, The monastical history of Ireland... Pp [29], 424. London: William Mears, 1722.

> Records much useful information, but the foundation dates for many Augustinian houses are wrong, owing to misinterpretation of Thomas Herrera, *Alphabetum Augustinianum* (2 vols, Madrid, 1644). Stevens' translation contains additions, but also omits detail included in the original. See F. X. Martin, 'The Augustinian friaries in pre-Reformation Ireland', **443**.

430 ARCHDALL (Mervyn). Monasticon Hibernicum; or, An history of the abbies, priories, and other religious houses in Ireland, interspersed with memoirs of their several founders and benefactors, and of their abbots and other superiors, to the time of their final suppression; likewise an account of the manner in which the possessions belonging to those foundations were disposed of, and the present state of their ruins; collected from English, Irish, and foreign historians, records, and other authentic documents, and from many curious and valuable manuscripts. With engravings of the several religious and military habits, and a map illustrating the history. Pp xxiii, 827. Dublin: Luke White; London: C. C. J. & J. Robinson, 1786; repr. [with notes by P. F. Moran and George Conroy] in *I.E.R.*, new ser., v (1868-9)-viii (1870-1), passim; Revised ed., edited by Patrick Francis Moran. Vols i, ii. Dublin: W. B. Kelly, 1873-6. *No more published.*

> Remains a valuable survey in spite of some inaccuracies and omissions, but now superseded by A. Gwynn and R. N. Hadcock, **432**.

431 GWYNN (Aubrey Osborn). Towards a new Monasticon Hibernicum. In *Ir. Cath. Hist. Comm. Proc.*, 1958, pp 24-8.

> A critical survey of comprehensive studies of Irish monasticism since the list in Sir James Ware, *De Hibernia et antiquitatibus eius disquisitiones* (1654; repr. in **128**). The projected work and map described on p. 28 have since been published, see **182, 432**.

432 GWYNN (Aubrey Osborn) *and* HADCOCK (Richard Neville). Medieval religious houses: Ireland. With an appendix to early sites. With a foreword by David Knowles. Pp xii, 479. London: Longman, 1970.

> An indispensable reference work for 5th-17th centuries, containing concise historical notes on each establishment, arranged under religious order. General introductory chapter, 'The origins and development of monas-

ticism in Ireland' (pp 1-12); short essays on early Irish monasteries, cathedrals, and each order. Thorough citation of sources throughout. Indexes of places and alternative placenames. Tables. Map: *Monastic Ireland*, 2nd ed., 1965, in pocket—see **182**.

433 LEE (Gerard Anthony). The leper hospitals of Munster. In *N. Munster Antiq. Jn.*, x (1966-7), 12-26.
An introductory account and annotated list.

434 MARTIN (Francis Xavier). The Irish friars and the observant movement in the fifteenth century. In *Ir. Cath. Hist. Comm. Proc.*, 1960, pp 10-16.
Analyses the causes and political significance of the movement in the Augustinian, Dominican and Franciscan orders.

435 O'SULLIVAN (Denis). Three little-known monastic establishments in mediaeval Cork. In *Féilscríbhinn Torna* (1947), pp 203-8.
Short historical accounts of the Benedictine priory of St John the Evangelist, the priory and leper hospital of St Stephen, and the preceptory of the Knights Hospitallers of St John of Jerusalem.

436 RICHARDSON (Henry Gerald). Some Norman monastic foundations in Ireland. In *Med. studies presented to A. Gwynn* (1961), pp 29-43.
Discusses the relationship between certain Irish and English houses, co-operation with early Anglo-Norman settlers, and pre-Cistercian reform movements.

(ii) Augustinians

437 BATTERSBY (William Joseph). A history of all the abbeys, convents, churches, and other religious houses of the Order, particularly of the Hermits, of St Augustine in Ireland, from the earliest period to the present time; with biographical sketches of the bishops, provincials, priors, etc. of that holy institute. Pp 286. Dublin: G. P. Warren, 1856.
A catalogue of Irish Augustinian houses, giving details of foundation, size, etc., dissolution, and subsequent fate of the buildings.

438 DUNNING (Patrick Joseph). The Arroasian Order in medieval Ireland. In *I.H.S.*, iv (1944-5), 297-315.
Concerned primarily with the continental origins of the order, and its introduction to Ireland in the twelfth century. See also **445**.

439 FLOOD (William Henry Grattan). The Premonstratensians in Ireland. In *I.E.R.*, 5th ser., ii (1913), 624-31.
A short account of each of the eleven Irish houses from 1180 to the 16th cent. For a fuller account see Norbert Backmund, *Monasticon Praemonstratense*, ii (Straubing: C. Attenkofersche, 1952), pp 119-52.

440 HADCOCK (Richard Neville). The Order of the Holy Cross in Ireland. In *Med. studies presented to A. Gwynn* (1961), pp 44-53.
A short, lucid account of the Irish houses in their European context.

441 HADCOCK (Richard Neville), The origin of the Augustinian Order in Meath. In *Ríocht na Midhe*, iii (1963-6), 124-31.
Includes material on the Anglo-Norman settlement.

442 MAC GIOLLA PHADRAIG (Brian). 14th century life in a Dublin monastery. In *Dublin Hist. Rec.*, vii (1944-5), 69-80.
Based on *Account roll of the priory of the Holy Trinity, Dublin, 1337-1346,* ed. James Mills (Dublin: R.S.A.I., 1891. Extra vol. for 1890-1).

443 MARTIN (Francis Xavier). The Augustinian friaries in pre-Reformation Ireland. In *Augustiniana* (Louvain: Institut historique des Augustins), vi (1956), 346-84.
A critical survey of the sources and a list of the 22 Irish houses, with detailed historical and bibliographical notes. Map.

444 MARTIN (Francis Xavier). The Irish Augustinian reform movement in the fifteenth century. In *Med. studies presented to A. Gwynn* (1961), pp 230-64.
Traces the development of the observant movement, with an introductory discussion of the Irish and continental background. Map.

445 WALSH (Timothy John) *and* O'SULLIVAN (Denis). Saint Malachy, the Gill Abbey of Cork, and the rule of Arrouaise. In *Cork Hist. Soc. Jn.*, liv (1949), 41-61.
Includes an examination of the extent of adoption of the Arroasian rule in medieval Ireland. See also P. J. Dunning, **438**.

(iii) Benedictines

446 BINCHY (Daniel Anthony). The Irish Benedictine congregation in medieval Germany. In *Studies*, xviii (1929), 194-210.

447 BROOKS (Eric St John). Irish daughter houses of Glastonbury. In *R.I.A. Proc.*, lvi (1953-4), C, no. 4 (1954), 287-95.
Examines the documentary evidence relating to the foundation of houses at Kilcommon, Co. Tipperary, and Ardaneer, Co. Limerick, *c*.1200.

448 GWYNN (Aubrey Osborn). The continuity of the Irish tradition at Würzburg. In *Herbipolis jubilans: 1200 Jahre Bistum Würzburg: Festschrift zur Säkularfeier der Erhebung der Kiliansreliquien* (Würzburg, 1952. Würzburger Diözesangeschichtsblätter, 14./15. Jahrgang, 1952/53), pp 57-81.

449 VAREBEKE (Hubert Janssens de). Benedictine bishops in medieval Ireland. In *North Munster studies* (1967), pp 242-50.
A brief biography of each prelate.

450 VAREBEKE (Hubert Janssens de). The Benedictines in medieval Ireland. In *R.S.A.I. Jn.*, lxxx (1950), 92-6.
A somewhat disjointed summary, but assembles useful factual information. Map.

(iv) Capuchins

451 MARTIN (Francis Xavier). Sources for the history of the Irish Capuchins. In *Collectanea Franciscana* (Roma: Istituto Storico dei Frati Minori Cappuccini), xxvi (1956), 67-79.

(v) Carmelites

452 GRAHAM (Paul). Carmelite bishops in Ireland. In *Zelo* (Gort Muire, Dundrum, Co. Dublin: Irish Province of the Order of Carmelites), ix (1957), 80-103.

453 McCAFFREY (Patrick Romaeus). The White Friars: an outline Carmelite history, with special reference to the English-speaking provinces. With a foreword by P. E. Magennis. Pp xx, 507. Dublin: Gill, 1926.
Includes chapters on the order in Ireland, 13th-15th centuries (pp 344-93). Plates.

454 MAGENNIS (Peter Elias). De Hiberniae Provincia. In *Analecta Ordinis Carmelitarum Derecto Capituli Generalis* (Roma: apud Curiam Generalitiam), i (1909-10), 387-92.

455 O'DWYER (Peter). The Carmelite Order in pre-Reformation Ireland. In *I.E.R.*, 5th ser., cx (1968), 350-63; repr. in *Ir. Cath. Hist. Comm. Proc.*, 1968, pp 49-62.
A concise, well-documented survey.

(vi) Carthusians

456 GRAY (Andrew). Kinaleghin: a forgotten Irish Charterhouse of the thirteenth century. In *R.S.A.I. Jn.*, lxxxix (1959), 35-58.
A well-documented account of the Carthusians in Ireland. Supersedes W. H. Grattan Flood, 'The Carthusians in Ireland: Kinalehin Priory, 1280-1321' in *I.E.R.*, 4th ser., xxii (1907), 304-9, and J. P. Dalton, 'The abbey of Kilnalahan' in *Galway Arch. Soc. Jn.*, vi (1909-10), 10-26, 65-94, 187-221, vii (1911-12), 103-14.

(vii) Cistercians

457 BROWN (Alfred Lawson). The Cistercian abbey of Saddell, Kintyre. In *The Innes Review* (Glasgow: John S. Burns), xx (1969), 130-7.
Includes discussion of its probable affiliation to Mellifont.

458 CONWAY (Colmcille). The abbatial succession at Mellifont, 1142-1539, by Father Colmcille, O.C.S.O. In *Louth Arch. Soc. Jn.*, xv (1961-4), 23-38.

459 CONWAY (Colmcille). Comhcheilg na Mainistreach Móire, [by] an tÁthair Colmcille, O.C.S.O. Pp 218. Baile Átha Cliath: Sáirséal agus Dill, 1968.
An account of 'the Mellifont conspiracy', expanding his section on this in *The story of Mellifont*, **465**. Based on the reports of Stephen of Lexington. See also B. W. O'Dwyer, **472**.

460 CONWAY (Colmcille). Decline and attempted reform of the Irish Cistercians, 1445-1531, [by] Fr M.-Colmcille, O.C.R. In *Collectanea Ordinis Cisterciensium Reformatorum* (Westmalle, Belgium: Abbaye des Trappistes), xviii (1956), 290-305; xix (1957), 146-62, 371-84.
A detailed study of the efforts to restore discipline and unity in the order after the Schism.

461 CONWAY (Colmcille). The lands of St Mary's Abbey, Dublin, by C. Ó Conbhuí. In *R.I.A. Proc.*, lxii (1961-3), C, no. 3 (1962), 21-84.
An important study of the development of a large monastic estate from its origins to the Dissolution. See also **462**.

462 CONWAY (Colmcille). The lands of St Mary's Abbey, Dublin, at the dissolution of the abbey: the demesne lands and the grange of Clonliffe, [by] Fr Colmcille, O.C.S.O. In *Reportorium Novum*, iii (1961-4), 94-107.
Demonstrates that the abbey's lands between the rivers Tolka and Liffey were more extensive than is indicated by the extent of 1540. See also **461**.

463 CONWAY (Colmcille). The origins of Jerpoint Abbey, Co. Kilkenny, [by] C. O'Conbhuidhe. In *Cîteaux: Commentarii Cistercienses* (Westmalle, Belgium: Abbaye des Trappistes), xiv (1963), 293-306.
An important re-examination, correcting earlier authorities.

464 CONWAY (Colmcille). Sources for the history of the Irish Cistercians, 1142-1540. In *Ir. Cath. Hist. Comm. Proc.*, 1958, pp 16-23.
A critical survey.

465 CONWAY (Colmcille). The story of Mellifont, by Father Colmcille, O.C.R. Pp lvii, 332. Dublin: Gill, 1958.

Includes much general information on the Cistercians in Ireland. His 'Irish Cistercians, 1140-1540', here (p 220, note 5) misleadingly cited as a book, has not yet been published as such, but some of it has subsequently appeared as articles—see **458, 466**. For later history, 1540-1752, see his 'Studies in Irish Cistercian history' in *Cîteaux*, xvi (1965), 5-28, 177-8, 257-77; xvii (1966), 5-24; xviii (1967), 38-50, 152-63; xix (1968), 326-50; xx (1969), 170-96.

466 CONWAY (Colmcille). Taxation of the Irish Cistercian houses, *c*.1329-1479, [by] Colmcille O'Conbhuidhe. In *Cîteaux: Commentarii Cistercienses* (Westmalle, Belgium: Abbaye des Trappistes), xv (1964), 144-60.

A detailed examination of the evidence for taxation by the Cistercian General Chapter. See also G. H. Orpen, 'Some Irish Cistercian documents' in *E.H.R.*, xxviii (1913), 303-13.

467 DE PAOR (Liam). Excavations at Mellifont Abbey, Co. Louth. In *R.I.A. Proc.*, lxviii (1969), C, no. 2, 109-64.

Report of the excavations of 1954-5, including a historical summary (pp 111-20). Appendices on special aspects by J. Hunt, H. J. Plenderleith, and Michael Dolley. Copiously illustrated with plans, drawings, and 26 plates.

468 GWYNN (Aubrey Osborn). The origins of St Mary's Abbey, Dublin. In *R.S.A.I. Jn.*, lxxix (1949), 110-25.

An account of its 12th-century origins and early history, in the context of Cistercian developments in the British Isles as a whole.

469 HEALY (John). The Cistercians in Ireland. In *I.E.R.*, 4th ser., ix (1901), 481-98.

A short introductory survey.

470 LEASK (Harold Graham). Irish Cistercian monasteries: a pedigree and distribution map. In *R.S.A.I. Jn.*, lxxviii (1948), 63-4.

Supplementary to A. H. Thompson, A. W. Clapham and H. G. Leask, 'The Cistercian Order in Ireland', **477**. Table shows the descent of daughter houses from Mellifont and foreign houses.

471 MAC NIOCAILL (Gearóid). Na manaigh liatha in Éirinn, 1142-*c*.1600. Pp xi, 246. Baile Átha Cliath: Cló Morainn, 1959.

A history of the Irish Cistercians to the Reformation, with a summary in French (pp 132-40). Bibliography, tables, map. It should be studied in conjunction with C. Conway, *The story of Mellifont*, **465**, which was published too late for consideration in this work; both are the products of important original research. See also the review by F. X. Martin in *I.H.S.*, xii (1959-60), 163-5, which includes a brief summary of Irish Cistercian historiography since the 17th century.

472 O'DWYER (Barry William). The conspiracy of Mellifont, 1216-1231: an episode in the history of the Cistercian order in medieval Ireland. Pp 47. [Dublin]: published for the Dublin Historical Association, 1970. (Medieval Irish history series, no. 2)

> A well-balanced, comprehensive study, summarising his unpublished Ph.D. thesis. Bibliographical note (pp 42-4). List and map of medieval Irish Cistercian monasteries by Colmcille Conway (pp 46-7). See also C. Conway, **459**.

473 O'DWYER (Barry William). Gaelic monasticism and the Irish Cistercians, *c*.1228. In *I.E.R.*, 5th ser., cviii (1967), 19-28; repr. in *Ir. Cath. Hist. Comm. Proc.*, 1965-7, pp 25-34.

> The survival of native Irish characteristics as revealed by the visitation of Stephen of Lexington.

474 O'DWYER (Barry William). The impact of the native Irish on the Cistercians in the thirteenth century. In *Jn. Relig. Hist.*, iv (1967) 287-301.

> Examines the conflict between Gaelic and continental cultures and traditions within the Irish Cistercian order. See also **473**.

475 O'DWYER (Barry William). The problem of reform in the Irish Cistercian monasteries and the attempted solution of Stephen of Lexington in 1228. In *Jn. Eccles. Hist.*, xv (1964), 186-91.

> Considers the incompatibility of Stephen's proposed intellectual standards with the educational facilities available to Irish novices, in the context of the Mellifont filiation and racial conflict. Includes a summary of the Cistercian administrative system and its problems.

476 POWER (Patrick). The Irish Cistercian abbeys. In *I.E.R.*, 5th ser., xxvii (1926), 23-35.

> A short popular account, with a list of houses.

477 THOMPSON (Alexander Hamilton), CLAPHAM (*Sir* Alfred William) *and* LEASK (Harold Graham). The Cistercian Order in Ireland. In *Arch. Jn.*, lxxxviii (1931), 1-36.

> History and list of houses by Thompson, with a discussion of the architectual remains by Clapham and Leask. Many photographs and plans. See also H. G. Leask, 'Irish Cistercian monasteries', **470**.

(viii) Cluniacs

478 FLOOD (William Henry Grattan). The Cluniacs in Ireland. In *I.E.R.*, 5th ser., i (1913), 52-9.

> A short history of the priory of Athlone—the only Cluniac house in Ireland—from its foundation in 1150 to the 15th century.

(ix) Dominicans

479 BURKE (Thomas). Hibernia Dominicana; sive, Historia provinciae Hiberniae ordinis praedicatorum . . . , per P. Thomam de Burgo. Pp xvi, 797. Coloniae Agrippinae (Köln): ex Typographia Metternichiana sub Signo Gryphi, 1762.
Supplementum. Pp 799-950. 1772.
General chronological account, followed by sections on individual houses.

480 KEARNS (Conleth). Medieval Dominicans and the Irish language. In *I.E.R.*, 5th ser., xciv (1960), 17-38.
A discussion of the evidence for the use of Gaelic by the Irish Dominicans, with a list of continental works—mainly of the 14th-15th centuries—translated into Gaelic at the time.

481 MACINERNY (M. Humbert). The Dominicans in Ireland. In *Miscellanea Dominicana in memoriam VII anni saecularis ab obitu Sancti Patris Dominici, 1221-1921* (Roma: apud Bibliopolam Franciscum Ferrari, 1923), pp 251-61.
A short historical survey from 1224 to 1920.

482 MACINERNY (M. Humbert). A history of the Irish Dominicans, from original sources and unpublished records. Vol. i. Irish Dominican bishops, 1224-1307. Pp xi, 635. Dublin, etc.: Browne & Nolan, 1916.
No more published.
Biographies of 13 prelates, containing much information on Irish ecclesiastical conditions.

483 MOULD (Daphne Desirée Charlotte Pochin). The Dominican Third Order: its history in Ireland. In *Ir. Rosary*, lx (1956), 225-30.
A history of the order since the first Irish foundations in the early 15th century. Very little evidence for the medieval period.

484 MOULD (Daphne Desirée Charlotte Pochin). The Irish Dominicans: the Friars Preachers in the history of Catholic Ireland. Pp xvii, 276. Dublin: Dominican Publications, 1957.
Includes chapters on the medieval period (pp 14-73). Photographs, plans and bibliography, but no detailed references.

485 O'SULLIVAN (Benedict). The coming of the friars. In *Ir. Rosary*, lii (1948), 165-70, 211-17, 283-8.
An account of the arrival of the Dominicans in Ireland and the social and religious background to their early foundations there, serving as an introduction to his 'Medieval Irish Dominican studies', **486**.

486 O'SULLIVAN (Benedict). Medieval Irish Dominican studies. In *Ir. Rosary*, lii (1948), 351-6; liii (1949), 39-44, 91-7, 154-9, 242-7, 304-9; liv (1950), 49-54, 86-92, 169-75, 224-30, 375-81; lv (1951), 37-44, 93-9, 167-75, 221-6, 281-6, 373-8; lvi (1952), 43-9, 107-12, 163-9, 219-25, 288-93, 356-63; lvii (1953), 21-8.

> A series of articles together with his 'The coming of the friars', **485,** forming the best comprehensive account, and a work of original scholarship.

487 RYAN (Finbar) *and* COLEMAN (Ambrose). The Dominicans in Ireland. In their *St Dominic & the Dominicans; and The Dominicans in Ireland, 1216-1916* (Dublin: Irish Rosary Office, 1916), pp 17-32.

> A brief historical survey.

(x) Franciscans

488 BLAKE (Martin Joseph). The Franciscan convents in Connacht, with notes thereon. In *Galway Arch. Soc. Jn.*, xiv (1928-9), 25-9.

> An annotated list, based on B. M. Sloane MS no. 4814.

489 CLEARY (Gregory). The Friars Minor in Dublin, 1232-1939. In *Assisi*, xi (1939), 346-9, 403-5, 455-8, 527-30; repr., with a foreword by Angelus Hollis. Pp [35]. Dublin: Assisi P., [1939].

> A short history, including a discussion of the origins of the order. Published anonymously for the consecration of the renovated Franciscan Church in Dublin.

490 CLEARY (Gregory). Saint Francis and Ireland. In *Studies*, xv (1926), 542-56; xvi (1927), 56-68, 413-24.

> The Franciscans in medieval Ireland.

491 FITZMAURICE (E. Bonaventure) *and* LITTLE (Andrew George), *ed.* Materials for the history of the Franciscan province of Ireland, A.D. 1230-1450. Pp xxxviii, 235. Manchester: Manchester U.P., 1920. (British Society of Franciscan Studies, ix); *repr.* Farnborough: Gregg P., 1966.

> Includes a historical introduction by A. G. Little (pp xi-xxxiv), lists of provincial ministers, chapters, and Franciscan bishops. Map.

492 MAC NIOCAILL (Gearóid). Uilliam Ó Raghallaigh, O.F.M. In *Irisleabhar Muighe Nuadhat* (Maynooth: St Patrick's College), 1961, pp 47-9.

> A 15th-century Irish Franciscan provincial.

493 MEEHAN (Charles Patrick). The rise and fall of the Irish Franciscan monasteries, and memoirs of the Irish hierarchy in the seventeenth century. With appendices containing original documents from the Rinuccini manuscripts, public records, and archives of the Franciscan Convent, Dublin. Pp xii, 252. Dublin, London: James Duffy, 1869; 5th ed. Pp iv, 504. [1877.]

> Includes the history of each house, based on the work of Fr Mooney, 1608. Originally published as a series of articles in *The Hibernian Magazine*.

494 MOONEY (Canice). The Franciscans in Ireland. In *Terminus* (Dublin: Sodality of Our Lady, C.I.E.), viii (1954), 66-9, 84-7, 105-8, 126-8, 150-3, 180-2; ix (1954), 193-5; x (1954), 226-8, 245-50; xi (1955), 5-9, 39-41, 85-9, 128-32; xii (1956), 14-17, 40-4; xiii (1956), 58-62, 88-92, 105-110, 139-44; xiv (1957), 13-17, 24, 28-40, 62-6, 87-9, 112-14.

> A series of articles comprising a valuable popular account of the Irish Franciscans from their arrival to the Reformation.

495 MOONEY (Canice). Irish Franciscan provincials. In *Archivum Franciscanum Historicum* (Quaracchi, Italy: Collegium S. Bonaventura), lvi (1963), 3-11.

> A list, with an introduction discussing the problems of its compilation, and methods of appointment.

(e) MILITARY ORDERS

(i) Knights Hospitallers

496 FALKINER (Caesar Litton). The Hospital of St John of Jerusalem in Ireland. In *R.I.A. Proc.*, xxvi (1906-7), C, no. 12 (1907), 275-317.
An account of the Irish possessions based on Kilmainham, and the significance of the order in Irish history. Appendices list Irish preceptories by county, and priors of Kilmainham, 1180-1557.

497 FALKINER (Caesar Litton). The Knights Hospitallers in Co. Galway. In *Galway Arch. Soc. Jn.*, iv (1905-6), 213-18.
A more detailed examination of the location of the hospital at Kinalekin (here identified as Kinal Ffeighin), supplementary to his 'The Hospital of St John of Jerusalem in Ireland', **496**.

498 MACDERMOTT (Anthony). The Knights of St John of Jerusalem in Ireland. In *Ir. Geneal.*, iii (1956-67), 2-16.
A history, with lists of houses and priors.

499 SHERLOCK (William). Knights Hospitallers in Co. Kildare. In *Kildare Arch. Soc. Jn.*, vi (1909-11), 89-95.

500 TIPTON (Charles Leon). The Irish Hospitallers during the Great Schism. In *R.I.A. Proc.*, lxix (1970), C, no. 3, 33-43.

(ii) Knights Templars

501 CULLEN (John B.). The coming of the Knights Templars to Ireland. In *I.E.R.*, 5th ser., xiv (1919), 24-37.
Mainly antiquarian notes.

502 MACINERNY (M. Humbert). The Templars in Ireland. In *I.E.R.*, 5th ser., ii (1913), 225-45.
Disagrees with H. Wood, **504**, on some points.

503 MACIVOR (Dermot). The Knights Templars in County Louth. In *Seanchas Ardmhacha*, iv (1960-1), 72-91.
Kilsaran Preceptory, *c.*1280-1314.

504 WOOD (Herbert). The Templars in Ireland. In *R.I.A. Proc.*, xxvi (1906-7), C, no. 14 (1907), 327-77.
The most detailed account of the privileges and activities of the order in Ireland, including the proceedings following its suppression in 1308. Appendices list territorial possessions by county.

(iii) Order of the Hospital of St Thomas of Acon

505 BROOKS (Eric St John). Irish possessions of St Thomas of Acre. In
R.I.A. Proc., lviii (1956-7), C, no. 2 (1956), 21-44.
Introduction (pp 21-8) discusses the origin of the order, and its two Irish
houses at Kilkenny and Carrickmagriffin, with their lands.

IX SOCIAL AND ECONOMIC HISTORY

(a) GENERAL

See also **181, 258, 268-71**

506 BERARDIS (Vincenzo). Italy and Ireland in the middle ages. Pp 227.
Dublin: Clonmore & Reynolds, 1950.
Considers the cultural and religious intercourse between the two countries,
431-*c*.1500. Introduction by John Ryan. Short bibliography; photographs of medieval buildings and paintings. See also Aubrey Gwynn,
513, and T. J. Westropp, **181**.

507 BLISS (Alan Joseph). The inscribed slates at Smarmore. In *R.I.A.
Proc.*, lxiv (1964-6), C, no. 2 (1965), 33-60.
A detailed study of slates bearing inscriptions probably originating in a
15th-century village school. 4 plates.

508 CHART (David Alfred). An economic history of Ireland. Pp ix, 210.
Dublin: Talbot P., 1920.
Includes chapters on the medieval period to 1485 (pp 1-24) and on
finance and currency (pp 151-84).

509 CULLEN (Louis Michael). Life in Ireland. Pp xiv, 178. London:
Batsford; New York: Putnam, 1968.
A popular but scholarly sketch, exceptionally well illustrated from contemporary sources. 'Conflict in Ireland: the old order and the new towns,
800-1550' (pp 20-49) is the best general account of the social and cultural
history of the period.

510 CURTIS (Edmund). The spoken languages of medieval Ireland. In
Studies, viii (1919), 234-54.
Examines the distribution and interaction of the principal languages
among the various population groups and regions. Based on documentary evidence.

511 FLEISCHMANN (Aloys Georg) *and* GLEESON (Ryta). Music in ancient
Munster and monastic Cork. In *Cork Hist. Soc. Jn.*, lxx (1965),
79-98.
Includes discussion of the scanty evidence for the Anglo-Norman period
(pp 95-8).

512 GREEN (Alice Sophia Amelia Stopford). The making of Ireland and its
undoing, 1200-1600. Pp xvi, 511. London: Macmillan, 1908; 2nd
ed. Pp xxiv, 573. 1909; *repr.* Dublin, London: Maunsel, 1920.
Especially valuable for education, trade, and Gaelic culture, but allowance
should be made for her biassed analysis of the effects of 16th-century
English policies.

513 GWYNN (Aubrey Osborn). Irish society in the fifteenth century. In *Iris Hibernia* (Fribourg, Switzerland: Hibernia Society, University of Fribourg), iii (1953-7), no. 5 (1957), 33-42.
> Broadcast by R.E. as a Thomas Davis lecture in the series 'Ireland and Renaissance Europe', 1954. Examines the intellectual contact between Ireland and continental countries, especially Italy, suggesting that Ireland's isolation from the Renaissance was due mainly to the weakness of townlife.

514 GWYNN (Aubrey Osborn). The medieval university of St Patrick's, Dublin. In *Studies*, xxvii (1938), 199-212, 437-54.
> A through examination of the 14th-century efforts to found an Irish university.

515 LUCAS (Anthony Thomas). Footwear in Ireland. In *Louth Arch. Soc. Jn.*, xiii (1952-6), 309-92.
> A comprehensive historical study.

516 LUCAS (Anthony Thomas). Irish folk life. In *A view of Ireland* (1957), pp 196-206.
> A useful introductory survey, including methods of study. Short bibliography lists some specialised articles.

517 LUCAS (Anthony Thomas). Irish food before the potato. In *Gwerin* (Denbigh: Gee), iii (1960-2), no. 2 (December 1960), 8-43.
> A detailed account of foodstuffs consumed in Ireland before the 17th century, based on documentary and archaeological evidence.

518 LUCAS (Anthony Thomas). The role of the National Museum in the study of Irish social history. In *Museums Journal* (London: Museums Association), lxv (1965), 112-21.
> A lecture delivered at the Dublin Conference of the Museums Association, 1965. Discusses the problems arising from the paucity of literary or visual evidence for Irish social history, and demonstrates how this can be offset by museum collections.

519 LUCAS (Anthony Thomas). Washing and bathing in ancient Ireland. In *R.S.A.I. Jn.*, xcv (1965), 65-114.
> A comprehensive study covering all periods.

520 MCINTOSH (Angus) *and* SAMUELS (Michael Louis). Prolegomena to a study of mediaeval Anglo-Irish. In *Medium Aevum*, xxxvii (1968), 1-11.
> Includes a hand-list of 43 documents and texts, mainly 15th-16th century.

521 STANFORD (William Bedell). Towards a history of classical influences in Ireland. In *R.I.A. Proc.*, lxx (1970), C, no. 3, pp 13-91.

522 WENT (Arthur Edward James). Irish monastic fisheries. In *Cork Hist. Soc. Jn.*, lx (1955), 47-56.

Fisheries owned or occupied by monasteries at the dissolution. More specialised articles on the history of Irish fisheries are referred to in the footnotes, and others by this author have appeared subsequently in *R.S.A.I. Jn.*, and elsewhere.

(b) GAELIC SOCIETY

523 BINCHY (Daniel Anthony). Celtic and Anglo-Saxon kingship: the O'Donnell lectures for 1967-8, delivered in the University of Oxford on 23 and 24 May 1968. Pp vii, 53. Oxford: Clarendon P., 1970.
Concerned mainly with Celtic kingship as described in the Irish law tracts.

524 BINCHY (Daniel Anthony). The linguistic and historical value of the Irish law tracts. In *Brit. Acad. Proc.*, xxix (1943), 195-227. (The Sir John Rhys Memorial Lecture, 1943)
An authoritative survey of Gaelic legal institutions.

525 BINCHY (Daniel Anthony). Some Celtic legal terms. In *Celtica*, iii (1956), 221-31.
Collocates and examines the Welsh and Irish evidence for the terminology concerning succession to kingship and officium pietatis.

526 HENCHY (Séamas). Fosterage in medieval Ireland. In *I.C.H.S. Bull.*, no. 44 (March 1946), 1-2.
Its extent and significance in the preservation of Gaelic autonomy before 1560.

527 HOGAN (James). The Irish law of kingship, with special reference to Ailech and Cenél Eoghain. In *R.I.A. Proc.*, xl (1931-2), C, no. 3 (1932), 186-254.
An important, detailed study of the institution, including succession lists covering the Anglo-Norman period. 7 genealogical tables.

528 JOYCE (Patrick Weston). A social history of ancient Ireland, treating of the government, military system, and law; religion, learning, and art; trades, industries, and commerce; manners, customs, and domestic life of the ancient Irish people. 2 vols. London, New York, Bombay: Longmans, Green, 1903; *abridged ed. as* A smaller social history of ancient Ireland .... Pp xxiv, 574. London, New York, Bombay: Longmans, Green; Dublin: Gill, 1906.
A pioneer study of Gaelic society which must now be used with great caution. Illustrated.

529 MACNEILL (E n). Celtic Ireland. Pp xv, 182. Dublin: Martin Lester; London: Leonard Parsons, 1921.
An important work for the understanding of Gaelic institutions, although primarily concerned with the pre-Norman period.

530 MacNeill (Eoin). Early Irish laws and institutions. Pp 152. Dublin: Burns, Oates & Washbourne, [1935].

An indispensable survey of the Celtic social and legal structure, and of the effects of the introduction of feudalism. No index.

531 MacNeill (Eoin). Prolegomena to a study of the *Ancient laws of Ireland*. With an introduction and footnotes by D. A. Binchy. In *Ir. Jurist*, new ser., ii (1967), 106-15.

532 O'Hanlon (John). Ancient Irish land tenures. In *I.E.R.*, 3rd ser., xi (1890), 235-41.

A brief study of the classes of Gaelic tenant and their obligations.

(c) ANGLO-IRISH RELATIONS

533   CURTIS (Edmund). The clan system among English settlers in Ireland. In *E.H.R.*, xxv (1910), 116-20.

A discussion of the evidence for hibernicisation in a writ of 1350 in Harris's Collectanea, N.L.I. For criticism of the use of the term 'clan' in this context see E. MacNeill, *Early Irish laws and institutions*, **530**, pp 5-55.

534   CURTIS (Edmund). Rental of the manor of Lisronagh, 1333, and notes on 'betagh' tenure in medieval Ireland. In *R.I.A. Proc.*, xliii (1935-7), C, no. 3 (1936), 41-76.

Contains an important discussion of betaghry (pp 62-76). See also G. Mac Niocaill, **541**, and L. Price, **547**.

535   GWYNN (Aubrey Osborn). Archbishop David MacCearbhaill and the petition for the grant of English law to the Irish, 1277-83. In *I.C.H.S. Bull.*, new ser., v (1956), no. 77 (Dec. 1956), 1-2.

Summary of **536**.

536   GWYNN (Aubrey Osborn). Edward I and the proposed purchase of English law for the Irish, c.1276-80. In *R. Hist. Soc. Trans.*, 5th ser., x (1960), 111-27.

A detailed examination of the Irish side of the question and of the career of Archbishop David MacCarwell of Cashel. See also J. Otway-Ruthven **545, 546**.

537   HAND (Geoffrey Joseph). The status of the native Irish in the lordship of Ireland, 1272-1331. In *Ir. Jurist*, new ser., i (1966), 93-115.

A comprehensive and authoritative survey. See also E. Curtis, **534**, G· Mac Niocaill, **541**, and L. Price, **547**.

538   JOHNSTON (William John). The first adventure of the common law. In *Law Quart. Rev.*, xxxvi (1920), 9-30.

The introduction of English law to Ireland.

539   LYDON (James Francis Michael). The problem of the frontier in medieval Ireland. In *Topic: a journal of the liberal arts* (Washington, Penn.: Washington and Jefferson College), 13 (*i.e.* vol. vii, 1967, [pt 1]), pp 5-22.

A stimulating discussion of the fluctuating barrier between feudal and Gaelic civilisations.

540 MacInerny (M. Humbert). Social Ireland, 1295-1303. In *I.E.R.*, 5th ser., xvii (1921), 390-403, 585-602.

An uncompleted series of stories of Anglo-Norman oppression, gleaned from *Calendar of the justiciary rolls; or, proceedings in the court of the justiciar of Ireland, [1295-1303]*, ed. James Mills (Dublin: H.M.S.O., 1905).

541 Mac Niocaill (Gearóid). The origins of the betagh. In *Ir. Jurist*, new ser., i (1966), 292-8.

A reassessment of the status of the betagh in Anglo-Irish law, conflicting in some respects with the views of G. J. Hand, **537**, and L. Price, **547**. See also criticism by J. Otway-Ruthven in *I.H.S.*, xvi (1968-9), 104-6.

542 Maitland (Frederic William). The introduction of English law into Ireland. In *E.H.R.*, iv (1889), 516-17; repr. in his *Collected papers*, ed. H. A. L. Fisher (Cambridge: Cambridge U.P., 1911), ii, pp 81-3.

543 Murphy (Bryan). The status of the native Irish after 1331. In *Ir. Jurist*, new ser., ii (1967), 116-38.

An examination of the evidence of printed sources for the ineffectiveness of the statute of 1331 granting equal status at law to both English and native Irish.

544 O'Dwyer (*Sir* Michael). The fusion of Anglo-Norman and Gael. In *Ir. Geneal.*, i (1937-42), 110-19.

Factors affecting the amalgamation of the two races during the middle ages. See also J. F. Lydon, **539**.

545 Otway-Ruthven (Annette Jocelyn). The native Irish and English law in medieval Ireland. In *I.H.S.*, vii (1950-1), 1-16.

Considers grants of the use of the common law to individual Irishmen, the legal position of the betagh and the free Irishman, responsibilities of kin and lord, the influence of Irish law on the Anglo-Irish courts, and the campaign for the extension of the common law to all the Irish. See also **546**, and A. Gwynn, **536**, G. J. Hand, **537**, and B. Murphy, **543**.

546 Otway-Ruthven (Annette Jocelyn). The request of the Irish for English law, 1277-80. In *I.H.S.*, vi (1948-9), 261-70. (Select Documents, vi)

Introduction (pp 261-6) contains discussion of the negotiations in detail and sets them in context. See also **545**, and A. Gwynn, **536**.

547 Price (Liam). The origin of the word *betagius*. In *Ériu*, xx (1966), 185-90.

A valuable study of the etymology and meaning of the term as found in medieval documents. Dr Price's view of the status of bíatach in law is criticised by G. Mac Niocaill in **541**.

(d) AGRICULTURE

548 AALEN (Frederick Herman Andreasen). The origin of enclosures in eastern Ireland. In *Irish geographical studies in honour of E. Estyn Evans*, ed. N. Stephens and R. E. Glasscock (Belfast: Department of Geography, The Queen's University, 1970), pp 209-23.
See also A. J. Otway-Ruthven, **560**.

549 BERRY (Henry Fitzpatrick). The manor of Mallow in the thirteenth century. In *R.S.A.I. Jn.*, xxiv (1894), 14-24.
Based on inquisitions of 1282 and 1298.

550 BROOKS (Eric St John). 14th century monastic estates in Meath: the Llanthony cells of Duleek and Colp. In *R.S.A.I. Jn.*, lxxxiii (1953), 140-9.
A detailed picture of a monastic grange, reconstructed from extents subsequently published in *The Irish cartularies of Llanthony Prima & Secunda*, ed. E. St J. Brooks (Dublin: Stationery Office, 1953. I.M.C.).

551 EVANS (Emyr Estyn). The flachter. In *U.J.A.*, 3rd ser., iv (1941), 82-7.
The push-plough.

552 EVANS (Emyr Estyn). Some survivals of the Irish openfield system. In *Geography*, xxiv (1939), 24-36.
Rundale communities in the Errigal district of Co. Donegal, displaying many survivals of medieval practices.

553 LEISTER (Ingeborg). Das Werden der Agrarlandschaft in der Grafschaft Tipperary, Irland. Pp 430. Marburg: im Selbstverlag des Geographischen Institutes der Universität Marburg, 1963. (Marburger Geographische Schriften, 18)
'Das Nebeneinander von Iren und Anglo-Normannen, 1172-1641' (pp 38-64) is a general survey of the social structure, serving as an introduction to the main part of the book, which deals with the 17th century and later. It is not based on original research and contains some errors of detail, but collocates a great deal of information hitherto dispersed. Bibliography (pp 387-92).

554 LUCAS (Anthony Thomas). Furze: a survey and history of its uses in Ireland. Pp [8], 204. Dublin: Educational Company of Ireland, for the Folklore of Ireland Society, 1958 [1960]. (*Béaloideas*, xxvi); *repr.* Pp [5], 204. Dublin: published for Ard-Mhúsaem na h-Éireann, National Museum of Ireland, by the Stationery Office, 1960.
A comprehensive examination of its significance in rural life. Very little evidence for the medieval period.

555 LUCAS (Anthony Thomas). Sea sand and shells as manure. In *Studies in folk life* (1969), pp 183-203.

A history of their use in Ireland, including a section on the 13th and 14th centuries (pp 185-6).

556 MCAULIFFE (J. J.). Ploughing by horses' tails. In *I.B.L.*, xxix (1943-5), 9-11.

An examination of 17th-century evidence, suggesting that reports of the practice then were fabricated.

557 MCENERY (Michael Joseph). Address on the state of agriculture and the standard of living in Ireland in the years 1240-1350. In *R.S.A.I. Jn.*, 1 (1920), 1-18.

A narrative statistical summary of evidence relating to supplies for English armies outside Ireland, and of *Account roll of the priory of the Holy Trinity, Dublin, 1337-1346*, ed. James Mills (Dublin: R.S.A.I., 1891. Extra vol. for 1890-1). Lengthy end-notes include discussion of Irish measures and the procedure of purveyors.

558 MILLS (James). Tenants and agriculture near Dublin in the fourteenth century. In *R.S.A.I. Jn.*, xxi (1890-1), 54-63.

A detailed study of agricultural conditions on the estates of the archbishop of Dublin, based on the evidence of manorial extents. Especially important for the study of betaghs and firmarii. See also **413**.

559 O'LOAN (John J.). The manor of Cloncurry, Co. Kildare, and the feudal system of land tenure in Ireland. In *Dept. Agric. Jn.*, lviii (1961), 14-36.

A reconstruction of a medieval manorial estate. Map and drawing.

560 OTWAY-RUTHVEN (Annette Jocelyn). Enclosures in the medieval period. In *Ir. Geography*, v (1964-8), no. 2 (1965), 35-6.

Summary of a paper read at a symposium on 'Enclosures in eastern Ireland', 1964. Indicates the extent and general characteristics of 'parks' in a predominantly openfield system. See also F. H. A. Aalen, **548**.

561 OTWAY-RUTHVEN (Annette Jocelyn). The organization of Anglo-Irish agriculture in the middle ages. In *R.S.A.I. Jn.*, lxxxi (1951), 1-13.

A detailed analysis of the evidence for the coexistence of the openfield strip system and larger, consolidated holdings, with a discussion of the system of cultivation, labour services, and the various classes of tenant. Map.

(e) TOWNS AND TRADE

562 BERRY (Henry Fitzpatrick). Catalogue of the mayors, provosts, and bailiffs of Dublin City, A.D. 1229 to 1447. In *R.I.A. Proc.*, xxviii (1909-10), C, no. 2 (1910), 47-61.

Chronological lists, with a short introduction on sources.

563 BERRY (Henry Fitzpatrick). The records of the Dublin gild of merchants, known as the Gild of the Holy Trinity, 1438-1671. In *R.S.A.I. Jn.*, xxx (1900), 44-68.

A description of their subject content, including information on the organisation and activities of the gild in the 15th century.

564 CARUS-WILSON (Eleanora Mary). Medieval merchant venturers: collected studies. Pp xxxii, 314. London: Methuen, 1954; *repr.* 1967. (University Paperbacks)

'The overseas trade of Bristol in the fifteenth century' (pp 1-97) includes a section on Ireland (pp 13-28). See also A. Gwynn, **566**.

565 EDWARDS (Robert Walter Dudley). The beginnings of municipal government in Dublin. In *Dublin Hist. Rec.*, i (1938-9), 2-10.

An authoritative survey of the growth of civic powers, considering Dublin in the context of English and continental cities.

566 GWYNN (Aubrey Osborn). Medieval Bristol and Dublin. In *I.H.S.*, v (1946-7), 275-86.

A review of *Bristol charters, 1378-1499*, ed. H. A. Cronne (Bristol: Bristol Record Society, 1946). Compares the medieval history of the two cities, and published work on them. See also E. M. Carus-Wilson, **564**.

567 HARDIMAN (James). The history of the town and county of the town of Galway, from the earliest period to the present time; embellished with several engravings; to which is added a copious appendix containing the principal charters and other original documents. Pp xvi, 320, lx. Dublin: W. Folds, 1820.

Ch. 3: 'From the Anglo-Norman invasion to the year 1484' (pp 43-66). See also M. D. O'Sullivan, **572, 573**.

568 HORE (Herbert Francis). History of the town and county of Wexford. Edited by Philip Herbert Hore. 6 vols. London: Elliot Stock, 1900-11.

Individual volumes are unnumbered, but have separate subtitles. Note especially *Old and New Ross* (1900). Includes many original documents. See also G. H. Orpen, **571**.

569 HUGHES (Thomas Jones). The origin and growth of towns in Ireland. In *University Rev.*, ii (1957-62), no. 7 (1960), 8-15.
A general survey to the 20th century, originally broadcast by R.E. as a Thomas Davis lecture in 1958.

570 MAC NIOCAILL (Gearóid). Na buirgéisí, XII-XV aois. 1 vol. in 2. Baile Átha Cliath: Cló Morainn, 1964.
Iml. ii consists of commentary, discussing the origin and development of towns in Ireland, their officers, government, jurisdiction, finance, wealth, and trade in the middle ages. Cf. James Tait, *The medieval English borough: studies on its origins and constitutional history* (Manchester: Manchester U.P., 1936; *repr.* 1969. Publications of the University of Manchester, no. 245; Historical Series, no. 70).

571 ORPEN (Goddard Henry). New Ross in the thirteenth century: an address delivered before the New Ross Literary Society. Pp 28. Dublin: Dublin U.P. for the author, 1911.
A valuable study of the foundation and early history of a Hiberno-Norman town and its commercial importance. See also H. F. Hore, **568**.

572 O'SULLIVAN (Mary Donovan). Old Galway: the history of a Norman colony in Ireland. Pp xii, 488. Cambridge: Heffer, 1942.
Sections on medieval history (pp 9-78) and on various aspects of town life (pp 351-467). Bibliography, plates, map. See also review by H. G. Richardson in *I.H.S.*, iv (1944-5), 361-7, which is especially important for the medieval period, and J. Hardiman, **567**.

573 O'SULLIVAN (Mary Donovan). Revenue and expenditure in a mediaeval Irish town. In *I.C.H.S. Bull.*, no. 16 (January 1942), 1-3.
A brief survey of the chief sources of income and items of expenditure in Galway, based mainly on late 15th-century corporation records.

574 O'SULLIVAN (William). The economic history of Cork city from the earliest times to the Act of Union. Pp [21], 110. Dublin: Educational Co. of Ireland; Cork: Cork U.P.; London, New York, Toronto: Longmans, Green, 1937.
Includes two excellent chapters on the period 1270-1500 (pp 16-57).

575 RUSSELL (Josiah Cox). Late-thirteenth-century Ireland as a region. In *Demography* (Chicago: Population Association of America), iii (1966), 500-12.
A somewhat hypothetical attempt to estimate the distribution of population in Irish cities, as an indication of the wealth and social integration of the country as a whole. Bases too much on unsubstantiated comparisons with England, and a misunderstanding of the significance of the term 'burgess' in the context of medieval Ireland. Short English and Spanish summaries. Appendix (pp 511-12) discusses 'Friar Michael Bernard's evidence about New Ross in A.D. 1265'.

576 WEBB (John Joseph). The guilds of Dublin. Pp 298. Dublin: Three Candles, 1929.

> Includes a chapter on the guild merchant in medieval and Tudor times (pp 1-50).

577 WEBB (John Joseph). Municipal government in Ireland: mediaeval and modern. Pp 280. Dublin: Talbot P., 1918.

> A factual account of urban administration. Chapters 1-6 (pp 1-81) are concerned with the medieval period, including discussion of the hundred court, civic revenue and expenditure, relations with the central government and native population, control of trade and industry. Main sources are listed, but no detailed references.

(f) DRESS

578 McCLINTOCK (Henry Foster). Old Irish and Highland dress, and that of the Isle of Man. Pp [14], 188. Dundalk: Dundalgan P., 1943; 2nd ed. 2 vols, *or* 2 vols in 1. 1950.

> Standard work on medieval Irish dress. See Máire MacNeill in *I.H.S.*, iv (1944-5), 117-19, and A. T. Lucas in *I.H.S.*, vii (1950-1), 299-301.

579 MACLEOD (Catriona). Fifteenth century vestments in Waterford. In *R.S.A.I. Jn.*, lxxxii (1952), 85-98.

> Detailed, illustrated description of the only collection that can be attributed to pre-Reformation Ireland, albeit of continental origin.

X HISTORY OF LITERATURE

(a) GAELIC

580 CARNEY (James). The Irish bardic poet: a study in the relationship of poet and patron, as exemplified in the persons of the poet Eochaidh Ó hEoghusa (O'Hussey) and his various patrons, mainly members of the Maguire family of Fermanagh. Pp 40. Dublin: Dolmen P., 1967. (New Dolmen Chapbooks, no. 4)

> See critical review by Cuthbert Mhág Craith in *Studia Celt.*, iv (1969), 133-6.

581 MURPHY (Gerard). Glimpses of Gaelic Ireland: two lectures. Pp 64. Dublin: Fallon, 1948.

> 'Warriors and poets in thirteenth-century Ireland' (pp 33-64) examines the Gaelic reaction to the Anglo-Norman invasions, as embodied in native heroic poetry.

582 MURPHY (John E.). The religious mind of the Irish bards. In *Féil-sgríbhinn Eóin Mhic Néill* (1940), pp 82-6.

> Discusses religious ideas expressed in bardic poetry, 1250-1650.

583 Ó CUÍV (Brian). Literary creation and Irish historical tradition. In *Brit. Acad. Proc.*, xlix (1965), 233-62.

> Considers the factual content of bardic literature.

584 Ó CUÍV (Brian), *ed.* Seven centuries of Irish learning, 1000-1700. Pp 151. [Dublin]: Stationery Office for R.E., 1961. (Thomas Davis lectures)

> Added title-page in Irish: *Léann na Gaeilge in Éirinn, 1000-1700.*
> Text of 9 lectures on subjects connected with literature and history, broadcast in 1958. Includes Gerard Murphy, 'Irish storytelling after the coming of the Normans' (pp 72-86); D. A. Binchy, 'Lawyers and chroniclers' (pp 58-71); and Francis Shaw, **600**.

585 Ó MUIRÍ (Réamonn). Slán agaibh: a fhir chumtha. In *Irisleabhar Muighe Nuadhat* (Maynooth: St Patrick's College), 1961, pp 65-78.

> A study of the position of the Irish bards, 14th-17th centuries.

586 QUIGGIN (Edmund Crosby). Prolegomena to the study of the later Irish bards, 1200-1500. In *Brit. Acad. Proc.*, v (1911-12), 89-143; *repr.* Pp 54. New York: Haskell House, 1967. [American Committee for Irish Studies. Reprints in Irish studies, no. 2]

> An introductory survey of bardic poetry.

(b) ANGLO·IRISH

587 CAHILL (Edward). Norman French and English languages in Ireland, 1170-1540.ʰIn *I.E.R.*, 5th ser., li (1938), 159-73.

Largely based on St J. D. Seymour, **594**, and E. Curtis, **510**, but also using some published documents.

588 ESPOSITO (Mario). A bibliography of the Latin writers of mediaeval Ireland. In *Studies*, ii (1913), 495-521.

Short notes on MSS and editions, and on secondary works, including sections on the 12th-15th centuries (pp 510-14). Supplements the lists in August Potthast, *Biblotheca historica medii aevi*, 2. Aufl. (2 vols, Berlin: W. Weber, 1896); Cyr Ulysse Joseph Chevalier, *Répertoire des sources historiques du moyen âge*, 2e éd. (2 vols, Paris: A. Picard, 1905-7); Maximilianus Manitius, *Geschichte der lateinischen Literatur des Mittelalters*, T. 1 (München: Beck, 1911. Handbuch der klassischen Altertums-Wissenschaft, herausgegeben von Iwan von Müller, Bd ix, Abt. 2, T. 1).

589 ESPOSITO (Mario). Notes on mediaeval Hiberno-Latin and Hiberno-French literature. In *Hermathena*, no. 36 (1910), 58-72.

Includes a brief account of Geoffrey of Waterford, d. *c.*1300 (pp 69-71).

590 ESPOSITO (Mario). Some further notes on mediaeval Hiberno-Latin and Hiberno-French literature. In *Hermathena*, no. 37 (1911), 325-33.

Includes notes on Hiberno-French poetry (pp 332-3).

591 FLOWER (Robin). Ireland and medieval Europe. In *Brit. Acad. Proc.*, xiii (1927), 271-303. (The Sir John Rhys Memorial Lecture, 1927); repr. in his *The Irish tradition* (Oxford: Clarendon P., 1947), pp 107-41.

Discusses the effects of external sources on the literature of medieval Ireland.

592 GWYNN (Aubrey Osborn). The origins of the Anglo-Irish theatre. In *Studies*, xxviii (1939), 260-74.

Analyses the evidence of Durham Roll 5822 for theatrical performances in Ireland *c.*1366, and reviews the evidence for 15th-century performances.

593 MOONEY (Canice). Some medieval writings of the Irish Franciscans. In *Ir. Lib. Bull.*, iii (1942), 16-18.

594 SEYMOUR (St John Drelincourt). Anglo-Irish literature, 1200-1582. Pp 170. Cambridge: Cambridge U.P., 1929.

A history of Anglo-Norman and English literature in Ireland from the Golliard poet-clerks to the Tudor era.

XI HISTORY OF SCIENCE AND TECHNOLOGY

595 BERRY (Henry Fitzpatrick). The water supply of ancient Dublin. In *R.S.A.I. Jn.*, xxi (1890-1), 557-73.
Includes the medieval system.

596 HORNELL (James). The curraghs of Ireland. In *Mariner's Mirror*, xxiii (1937), 74-83, 148-75; xxiv (1938), 5-39; repr. in his *British coracles and Irish curraghs* (London: Quaritch, for the Society for Nautical Research, 1938), with the original mixed pagination.
The first detailed account of their history and construction, including local variants. Photographs and drawings.

597 LUCAS (Anthony Thomas). The dugout canoe in Ireland: the literary evidence. In *Varbergs Museum Arsbok* (Varberg), 1963, pp 57-68.
Notes medieval references to 'cots' or 'coite' (pp 57-60).

598 LUCAS (Anthony Thomas). The horizontal mill in Ireland. In *R.S.A.I. Jn.*, lxxxiii (1953), 1-36.
A comprehensive study, with detailed descriptions of individual examples. Includes a list of all known or probable sites, with bibliographical references; to this should now be added Edward M. Fahy, 'A horizontal mill at Mashanaglass, Co. Cork' in *Cork Hist. Soc. Jn.*, lxi (1956), 13-57, and his popular account of the same site, 'The genius of our Irish fore-fathers' in *Biatas: the beet grower* (Dublin: Cómhlucht Siúicre Éireann Teo), xi (1957-8), 401-6.

599 POLLOCK (A. J.) *and* WATERMAN (Dudley Mark). A medieval pottery kiln at Downpatrick. In *U.J.A.*, 3rd ser., xxvi (1963), 79-104.
A well-illustrated excavation report, describing a late 13th-early 14th century kiln and pottery remains, and discussing their evidence on technical processes.

600 SHAW (Francis). Irish medical men and philosophers. In *Seven centuries of Irish learning* (1961), pp 87-101.
Concerned mainly with medieval medicine.

601 SHAW (Francis). Medicine in Ireland in mediaeval times. In *What's past is prologue* (1952), pp 10-14.
Summarises the problems of adopting the new continental medical learning in Ireland after the Anglo-Norman invasion.

602 SHAW (Francis). Medieval medico-philosophical treatises in the Irish language. In *Féil-sgríbhinn Eóin Mhic Néill* (1940), pp 144-57.
A list of texts with notes on their content and character.

XII HISTORY OF FINE ART

603 ARNOLD (Bruce). A concise history of Irish art. Pp 216. London: Thames & Hudson, 1969. [World of Art Library. History of Art] 'From the Viking invasions to 1700' (pp 45-66). Well illustrated.

604 GRAVES (James). Ancient Irish stained glass. In *Kilkenny Arch. Soc. Trans.* [i.e. *R.S.A.I. Jn.*], i (1849-51), 210-14.
Concerned primarily with glass found at St Canice's Cathedral, Kilkenny, but includes a discussion of the general characteristics of 14th-century painted glass.

605 HENRY (Françoise). Irish art in the romanesque period, 1020-1170 A.D. Pp xvi, 240. London: Methuen, 1970; *originally published in French as her* L'art irlandais. T. iii. Pp 303. Sainte-Marie de la Pierre-qui-Vire, Yonne: Zodiaque, 1964. (Collection La Nuit des Temps, 20)

606 HENRY (Françoise). Irish Cistercian monasteries and their carved decoration. In *Apollo*, lxxxiv (1966), 260-7.
Illustrated analysis.

607 HENRY (Françoise). La sculpture irlandaise pendant les douze premiers siècles de l'ère chrétienne. 2 vols. Paris: E. Leroux, 1933. (Etudes d'Art et d'Archéologie, sous la direction d'Henri Focillon)
Text illustrated by drawings; volume of plates.

608 HENRY (Françoise) *and* MARSH-MICHELI (Geneviève Louise). A century of Irish illumination, 1070-1170. In *R.I.A. Proc.*, lxii (1961-3), C, no. 5 (1962), 101-64.
A thorough study of the style that became typical for the Anglo-Norman period. Map; 44 plates.

609 LAWLOR (Hugh Jackson). The monuments of the pre-Reformation archbishops of Dublin. In *R.S.A.I. Jn.*, xlvii (1917), 109-38.
A description of the brasses and other effigies, revealing characteristics apparently peculiar to Irish craftsmen. 12 plates.

610 MACLEOD (Catriona). Mediaeval wooden figure sculptures in Ireland: mediaeval madonnas in the west. In *R.S.A.I. Jn.*, lxxv (1945), 167-82.—Mediaeval figure sculpture in Ireland: statues in the Holy Ghost Hospital, Waterford. In *R.S.A.I. Jn.*, lxxvi (1946), 89-100.—Some mediaeval wooden figure sculptures in Ireland: statues of Irish saints. In *R.S.A.I. Jn.*, lxxvi (1946), 155-70.—Some late mediaeval wood sculptures in Ireland. In *R.S.A.I. Jn.*, lxxvii (1947), 53-62.
Detailed, illustrated descriptions of the rare surviving specimens.

611 RAE (Edwin C.). Irish sepulchral monuments of the later middle ages. Pt i. The Ormond group. In *R.S.A.I. Jn.*, c (1970), 1-38.
16 plates.

612 RAE (Edwin C.). The sculpture of the cloister of Jerpoint Abbey. In *R.S.A.I. Jn.*, xcvi (1966), 59-91.
An important contribution to the study of Irish gothic sculpture. 12 plates.

613 ROE (Helen Maybury). Cadaver effigial monuments in Ireland. In *R.S.A.I. Jn.*, xcix (1969), 1-19.
A study of a style current in Ireland from 15th to 17th centuries.

614 ROE (Helen Maybury). Medieval fonts of Meath. Pp [6], 128. [Navan]: Meath Archaeological & Historical Society, 1968.
An illustrated gazetteer, with definitive descriptions of all known examples.

615 ROE (Helen Maybury). Some aspects of medieval culture in Ireland. In *R.S.A.I. Jn.*, xcvi (1966), 105-9.
Surveys the research problems and opportunities afforded by sculptural remains. 10 plates.

XIII HISTORY OF ARCHITECTURE

(a) GENERAL

616 LEASK (Harold Graham). The characteristic features of Irish architecture from early times to the twelfth century. In *N. Munster Antiq. Jn.*, i (1936-9), 10-21.
Illustrated notes.

617 PHIPPS (Charles Benjamin). The problem of dating ancient Irish buildings. In *Hermathena*, no. 54 (1939), 54-92.
Concerned mainly with the pre-Norman period, but contains much technical information of general interest.

(b) ECCLESIASTICAL

618 CHAMPNEYS (Arthur Charles). Irish ecclesiastical architecture, with some notice of similar or related work in England, Scotland and elsewhere. With numerous illustrations, chiefly from photographs by the author. Pp xxiii, 258; 116 plates. London: G. Bell; Dublin: Hodges, Figgis, 1910; *repr., with a critical introduction by Liam de Paor.* Pp xxxiv, 258; 114 plates. Shannon: Irish U.P., 1970.

A detailed, comprehensive history to the 16th century, expanded from articles in *Architectural Review*, xvii (1905)-xxii (1907).

619 CLAPHAM (Sir Alfred William). Some minor Irish cathedrals. In *Medieval studies in memory of A. Kingsley Porter,* ed. Wilhelm R. W. Koehler (Cambridge, Mass.: Harvard U.P., 1939), ii, pp 699-708.

Superseded by **620.**

620 CLAPHAM (Sir Alfred William). Some minor Irish cathedrals. In *Memorial volume to Sir Alfred Clapham* (London: Royal Archaeological Institute of Great Britain and Ireland, 1952. *Arch. Jn.,* cvi, 1949, suppl.), pp 16-39.

Extended version of **619.** Individual architectural descriptions—edited by H. G. Leask and C. A. Ralegh Radford where left incomplete by the author. Well illustrated; plans by Vera M. Dallas.

621 DU NOYER (George Victor). Notes on some peculiarities in ancient and mediaeval Irish ecclesiastical architecture. In *Kilkenny Arch. Soc. Jn.,* new ser., v [i.e. *R.S.A.I. Jn.,* viii] (1864-6), 27-40.

Discusses the development of certain features. 16 text drawings; 4 plates.

622 LEASK (Harold Graham). The architecture of the Cistercian Order in Ireland in the XIIth and early XIIIth centuries. In *N. Munster Antiq. Jn.,* i (1936-9), 132-41.

Well-illustrated description of characteristic buildings, based on Jerpoint Abbey.

623 LEASK (Harold Graham). Irish churches and monastic buildings. 3 vols. Dundalk: Dundalgan P., 1955-60.

i. *The first phases and the romanesque.*
ii. *Gothic architecture to A.D. 1400.*
iii. *Medieval gothic: the last phases.*
The definitive study, by a professional architect and Inspector of National Monuments. Numerous photographs and informative drawings; 2 glossaries.

624 MᴄNᴇɪʟʟ (Charles). The affinities of Irish romanesque architecture. In *R.S.A.I. Jn.*, xlii (1912), 140-7.

Examines the written evidence for the influence of German ecclesiastical architecture on Ireland in the 11th and 12th centuries.

625 Mᴏᴏɴᴇʏ (Canice). Franciscan architecture in pre-Reformation Ireland. In *R.S.A.I. Jn.*, lxxxv (1955), 133-73; lxxxvi (1956), 125-69; lxxxvii (1957), 1-38, 103-24.

A comprehensive survey of characteristic features, illustrated by photographs, plans and drawings. Map.

626 Pʀɪᴍ (John G. A.). Observations on sedilia in Irish churches. In *Kilkenny Arch. Soc. Trans.* [i.e. *R.S.A.I. Jn.*], i (1849-51), 51-8.

An illustrated discussion of the recessed seats in some medieval chancels and of the armorial shields over them.

(c) MILITARY

627 FLEMING (James Stark). Irish and Scottish castles and keeps contrasted. In *R.S.A.I. Jn.*, xxxix (1909), 174-91.

An illustrated comparison of some typical examples.

628 FLEMING (James Stark). The town-wall fortifications of Ireland. Pp 90. Paisley: Alexander Gardiner, 1914.

Descriptions and historical notes on some surviving remnants, including Anglo-Norman. Sketches.

629 HICKEY (Elizabeth). Some observations on the usage of the word 'mote' in mediaeval times. In *Ríocht na Midhe*, ii (1959-62), no. 2 (1960), 37-9.

A note on its provenance in medieval writings, with special reference to Ireland.

630 JOPE (Edward Martyn) *and* SEABY (Wilfred Arthur). A new document in the Public Record Office: defensive houses in medieval towns. In *U.J.A.*, 3rd ser., xxii (1959), 115-18.

Short introduction by Jope (pp 115-6) discusses two towers and embattled houses in 14th-century Dublin.

631 KNOX (Hubert Thomas). The croghans and some Connacht raths and motes. In *R.S.A.I. Jn.*, xli (1911), 93-116.—Some Connacht raths and motes. In *R.S.A.I. Jn.*, xli (1911), 205-40, 301-42.

A detailed, illustrated account. See also criticism by G. H. Orpen in **636**.

632 LAWLOR (Henry Cairnes). Mote and mote-and-bailey castles in de Courcy's principality of Ulster. In *U.J.A.*, 3rd ser., i (1938), 155-64; ii (1939), 46-54.

An account of each castle in its historical context. Valuable also for the history of de Courcy's conquest. 2 maps.

633 LEASK (Harold Graham). Irish castles, 1180 to 1310. In *Arch. Jn.*, xciii (1936), 143-99.

Text largely superseded by his later work, **634**, but includes additional bibliographical information, plans and plates.

634 LEASK (Harold Graham). Irish castles and castellated houses. Pp [8], 170. Dundalk: Dundalgan P., 1941; 2nd ed. 1944.

The best account of the development of the Irish castle from the 12th century onwards, with an introductory chapter on its functions and parts, and weapons of siege and defence. The more important castles are listed by county, with a note on the total number. Glossary, numerous drawings (including architectural details), plans, 7 plates, map. See also **633**.

635 MORRIS (Henry). Motes and their origin. In *Louth Arch. Soc. Jn.*, ii (1908-11), 41-4.

Propounds the theory of Milesian origin. Cf. G. H. Orpen, **636-40**.

636 ORPEN (Goddard Henry). Croghans and Norman motes. In *R.S.A.I. Jn.*, xli (1911), 267-76.

Supplements his earlier papers on the origin of motes, **637, 638, 639, 640**, replying to and criticising H. T. Knox, **631**.

637 ORPEN (Goddard Henry). Motes and Norman castles in County Louth. In *R.S.A.I. Jn.*, xxxviii (1908), 241-69.

Illustrated. See note on **638**.

638 ORPEN (Goddard Henry). Motes and Norman castles in Ireland. In *R.S.A.I. Jn.*, xxxvii (1907), 123-52.

The first statement of his important Norman theory of the origin of motes, criticising T. J. Westropp's 'prehistoric theory' in **642, 643, 644**. For the subsequent development of Orpen's theory see **636, 637, 639, 640**.

639 ORPEN (Goddard Henry). Motes and Norman castles in Ossory. In *R.S.A.I. Jn.*, xxxix (1909), 313-42.

Examines the relationship between the principal motes and the earliest Anglo-Norman manors. See note on **638**.

640 ORPEN (Goddard Henry). The origin of Irish motes. In *Louth Arch. Soc. Jn.*, ii (1908-11), 50-6.

See note on **638**.

641 POWER (Patrick). The town wall of Waterford. In *R.S.A.I. Jn.*, lxxiii (1943), 118-36.

Describes the ruins of the Danish and Anglo-Norman walls and other fortifications. Pen-and-ink drawings by Robert Burke; plan by David Sheedy.

642 WESTROPP (Thomas Johnson). Irish motes and alleged Norman castles: note on some recent contributions to their study. In *R.S.A.I. Jn.*, xxxv (1905), 402-6.

Criticism of E. S. Armitage and others.

643 WESTROPP (Thomas Johnson). On Irish motes and early Norman castles. In *R.S.A.I. Jn.*, xxxiv (1904), 313-45.

An examination of the origin of motes, suggesting that all were pre-Norman. For a refutation of this view see G. H. Orpen, **638**.

644 WESTROPP (Thomas Johnson). The principal ancient castles of the County Limerick. In *R.S.A.I. Jn.*, xxxvii (1907), 24-40, 153-64.

Pt 1 deals with the medieval period. Illustrated.

(d) DOMESTIC

645 AALEN (Frederick Herman Andreasen). The evolution of the traditional house in western Ireland. In *R.S.A.I. Jn.*, xcvi (1966), 47-58.
Traces the development of the modern peasant dwelling from the primitive clochan. Drawings.

646 DANAHER (Kevin). Hearth and chimney in the Irish house, [by] Caoimhín Ó Danachair. In *Béaloideas*. xvi (1946), 91-104.
Examines the evolution of the various types. Photographs and drawings.

647 DANAHER (Kevin). Representations of houses on some Irish maps of *c.*1600, by Caoimhín Ó Danachair. In *Studies in folk life* (1969), pp 91-103.
Examines the illustrations of houses on the maps by Richard Barthelet reproduced in *Ulster and other Irish maps*, **183**. 8 plates.

648 EVANS (Emyr Estyn). Sod and turf houses in Ireland. In *Studies in folk life* (1969), pp 79-90.
A general study, illustrated by drawings and photographs of modern examples.

649 LUCAS (Anthony Thomas). Wattle and straw mat doors in Ireland. In *Arctica: essays presented to Ake Campbell, 1.5.1956*, ed. Arne Furumark [and others] (Uppsala: printed by Almqvist & Wiksells, 1956. Studia Ethnographica Upsaliensis, xi), pp 16-35.
A detailed analysis of the evidence, concluding that such doors were in continuous use from pre-Norman times.

650 Ó RÍORDÁIN (Seán Pádraig) *and* HUNT (John). Mediaeval dwellings at Caherguillamore, Co. Limerick. In *R.S.A.I. Jn.*, lxxii (1942), 37-63.
Report of the first excavation of a medieval dwelling site in Ireland—two houses, believed to have been occupied in 14th-16th centuries. A number of implements, etc. found on the site are illustrated.

XIV ARCHAEOLOGY

651 ANCIENT MONUMENTS ADVISORY COUNCIL FOR NORTHERN IRELAND. A preliminary survey of the ancient monuments of Northern Ireland, conducted by the Ancient Monuments Advisory Council for Northern Ireland. Edited by D. A. Chart. Pp xxiv, 284; 73 plates. Belfast: H.M.S.O., 1940.

> Adviser for prehistoric monuments: E. Estyn Evans; adviser for historic monuments of Antrim and Down: H. C. Lawlor.
> Short descriptions of individual monuments arranged by county, with introductory matter, glossary, plans, photographs, and an index map to the Ordnance Survey of Northern Ireland. Separate map in wallet shows the location of monuments; scale: ¼ inch: 1 mile.

652 ARCHAEOLOGICAL SURVEY OF NORTHERN IRELAND. An archaeological survey of County Down. Pp xxiv, 478; 213 plates. Belfast: H.M.S.O., 1966.

> The first volume of a projected series to cover all 6 counties of Northern Ireland. The section on 'Early Christian and medieval monuments and antiquities' (pp 101-312) contains a historical introduction, discussion of the various types of remains, and detailed individual descriptions. Many drawings, plans and photographs. Select bibliography; glossary.

653 BÓRD FÁILTE ÉIREANN. National monuments of Ireland in the charge of the Commissioners of Public Works in Ireland. Pp xxx, 116. Dublin: Bórd Fáilte Éireann, 1964.

> Also published in French and German translations. A useful list designed primarily for the tourist. Monuments are arranged by registered number, with brief descriptions. O.S. map reference, and bibliographical references to more detailed descriptions. Alphabetical index. Maps and drawings. Superseded by P. Harbison, **659**.

654 CHART (David Alfred). Air photography in Northern Ireland. In *Antiquity*, iv (1930), 453-9.

> An early account of its application to archaeology, not directly concerned with the medieval period. 7 photographs. See also J. K. St Joseph, **670**.

655 COMMISSIONERS OF PUBLIC WORKS IN IRELAND. Annual report, 1st- , 1832- . London: H.M.S.O., 1833- .

> Title varies: occasionally *Report*.
> Issuing body called Board of Public Works, 1839-74, and also called Choimisineiri na n-Oibreacha Puibli (*or* Poiblidhe), 1922- .
> Imprint varies: 90th- , 1921/22- , Dublin: Stationery Office, 1922- ; 1st-89th, 1832-1920, published as command papers. Includes descriptions of national monuments vested in the commission, some of which have also been published separately as *Extracts from the Annual reports of the Commissioners of Public Works in Ireland* (Dublin: H.M.S.O., 1905-). See also **667**.

656 COMMISSIONERS OF PUBLIC WORKS IN IRELAND. National monuments in charge of the Commissioners of Public Works, Ireland. Pp 29. Dublin: H.M.S.O., 1878.
Ecclesiastical buildings vested in 1869. Illustrated. See also **662, 668**.

657 DAVIES (Oliver). A summary of the archaeology of Ulster. In *U.J.A.*, 3rd ser., xi (1948), 1-42; xii (1949), 43-76.
Also published separately as an offprint. Synopsis of a lecture course for the Workers' Educational Association, Armagh, 1946-7. An excellent concise account, containing several plans and photographs. Includes 'The Norman conquest: castles' (pp 56-64); 'Medieval churches' (pp 64-70); 'Medieval sculpture' (pp 70-3).

658 GROSE (Francis). The antiquities of Ireland. 2 vols. London: S. Hooper, 1791 [i.e. 1795].
Published posthumously, with a preface by Edward Ledwich dated 1794; some plates are dated 1795.

659 HARBISON (Peter). Guide to the national monuments in the Republic of Ireland, including a selection of other monuments not in state care. Pp [16], 284. Dublin: Gill & Macmillan, 1970.
Cover title: *Guide to the national monuments of Ireland.*
A comprehensive list with a short description of each monument. Bibliographical notes. Maps, photographs, sketches. Supersedes **653**.

660 JOPE (Edward Martyn). Historic monuments. In *Belfast in its regional setting* (1952), pp 109-18.
Includes a survey of medieval remains in Ulster (pp 109-13).

661 LEASK (Harold Graham). A concise guide to ancient Irish structures; for the use of all interested in the preservation and recording of the remains of the past in Ireland. Issued by the Office of Public Works, Dublin. Pp 12. Dublin: Stationery Office, [1945].
At head of title: National monuments.
Published anonymously. See also **662, 668.**

662 LEASK (Harold Graham). The national monuments of the Irish Free State. Pp 31. Dublin: Stationery Office, [1936].
At head of title: Seadchómharthaí náisiúnta Shaorstáit Éireann.
Published anonymously. See also **661, 668.**

663 LEDWICH (Edward). Antiquities of Ireland. Pp viii, 486. Dublin: Arthur Grueber, 1790; 2nd ed., with additions and corrections, to which is added A collection of miscellaneous antiquities. Pp [20], 548. Dublin: John Jones, 1804.

664 MINISTRY OF FINANCE, *Northern Ireland.* Ancient monuments of Northern Ireland: an account of certain ancient monuments in the public charge. Pp 24. Belfast: H.M.S.O., 1926; 2nd ed. *as* An account of the ancient monuments in state charge. Pp 49. 1928; 3rd ed. Pp 76. 1947; 4th ed. *as* Ancient monuments of Northern Ireland. Vol i. In state care. Pp 114. 1962; 5th ed. Pp 132. 1966.

> Short descriptions of each monument, illustrated by drawings and photographs of a representative selection. See also **665, 666**.

665 MINISTRY OF FINANCE, *Northern Ireland.* Ancient monuments of Northern Ireland not in state care. Pp 64. Belfast: H.M.S.O., 1952; 2nd ed. *as* Ancient monuments of Northern Ireland. Vol. ii. Not in state care. Pp 80. 1963.

> An annotated list of monuments, with a general introductory account of archaeology and architecture in Ulster by E. M. Jope (2nd ed., pp 7-41). Map. See also **664, 666**.

666 MINISTRY OF FINANCE, *Northern Ireland.* [Guides to monuments in state care.] Belfast: H.M.S.O., 1928- .

> Illustrated pamphlets by experts, describing individual monuments in their historical context. A convenient, frequently revised list is contained in *Ancient monuments and historic buildings* (London: H.M.S.O. 1970- . Government Publications. Sectional List, no. 27). See also **664, 665**.

667 OFFICE OF PUBLIC WORKS, *Ireland.* Ancient and national monuments, Ireland. Baile Átha Cliath: Oifig an tSoláthair, 1925- .

> Title varies: *Seadchómharthaí náisiúnta na hÉireann.* Also known as 'National monuments pamphlets'.
> Issuing body varies: National Monuments Branch, Office of Public Works. Historical and descriptive notes on individual monuments, mainly extracted from *Annual reports of the Commissioners of Public Works in Ireland*, **655**. Most of the medieval pamphlets are by H. G. Leask. See also **666, 668**.

668 OFFICE OF PUBLIC WORKS, *Ireland.* Irish antiquities: general guide. Pp 19. Dublin: Stationery Office, [1962].

> An invaluable introduction to the various types of antiquity, explaining technical terms with the aid of excellent drawings. Revised edition of H. G. Leask, *A concise guide to ancient Irish structures*, **661**.

669 Ó RÍORDÁIN (Seán Pádraig). Antiquities of the Irish countryside. Pp xiv, 108. London: Methuen, 1942; 4th ed. 1964.

> Concerned primarily with pre-Norman remains, but includes a useful account of later medieval mottes.

670 ST JOSEPH (John Kenneth Sinclair). Air reconnaissance: recent results, 16. In *Antiquity*, xliii (1969), 57-9.

A report of recent work in Ireland and its implications. Some results, mainly concerning the pre-Norman period, have since been published in E. R. Norman and J. K. St Joseph, *The early development of Irish society: the evidence of aerial photography* (Cambridge: Cambridge U.P., 1969. Cambridge Air Surveys, iii).

671 WAKEMAN (William Frederick). A handbook of Irish antiquities, pagan and Christian, especially of such as are easy of access from the Irish metropolis. Pp xviii, 176. Dublin: James McGlashan, 1848; 2nd ed. Dublin: McGlashan & Gill, 1858; 3rd ed., by John Cooke. Pp xvi, 414. Dublin: Hodges, Figgis; London: John Murray, 1903.

1st ed. has at head of title: Archaeologia Hibernica. Subtitle varies slightly in subsequent editions. Includes 'Anglo-Irish remains' (1st ed., pp 109-46).

XV NUMISMATICS

Only the more important general and introductory works are listed here. Many specialised articles will be found in periodicals, in particular *British Numismatic Journal, Numismatic Chronicle, Seaby's Coin and Medal Bulletin,* and *Spink's Numismatic Circular.* A critical bibliography is included in M. Dolley, *Mediaeval Anglo-Irish coins,* to be published in 1971.

672 COFFEY (George). Catalogue of Irish coins in the collection of the Royal Irish Academy, Science and Art Museum, Dublin. Pt. 2. Anglo-Irish. Pp 123. Dublin: Department of Science and Art of the Committee of Council on Education, 1895.

673 DOLLEY (Reginald Hugh Michael). Anglo-Irish monetary policies, 1172-1637. In *Hist. Studies,* vii (1969), 45-64.
Investigates why coins were struck at particular times.

674 DOLLEY (Reginald Hugh Michael). The Irish mints of Edward I in the light of the coin-hoards from Ireland and Great Britain. In *R.I.A. Proc.,* lxvi (1967-8), C, no. 3 (1968), 235-97.

675 DOLLEY (Reginald Hugh Michael) *and* PAGAN (Hugh). Great Britain and Ireland. In *A survey of numismatic research, 1960-1965,* ed. Kolbjorn Skaare and George C. Miles (Copenhagen: International Numismatic Commission, 1967), ii, *Medieval and oriental numismatics,* pp 174-202.
A narrative bibliography of published work, including a section on Ireland by Dolley (pp 199-202).

676 DOLLEY (Reginald Hugh Michael) *and* SEABY (Wilfred Arthur). Anglo-Irish coins: John-Edward III, Ulster Museum, Belfast. Pp lvii, [33]; 16 plates. London: Oxford U.P., for the British Academy and the Trustees of the Ulster Museum, 1968. (Sylloge of Coins of the British Isles, C [1], pt 1 [Consecutive series, 10])

677 DOWLE (Anthony) *and* FINN (Patrick). The guide book to the coinage of Ireland from 995 A.D. to the present day. Foreword by Michael Dolley. Pp 127. London: Spink, 1969.
An illustrated catalogue of all known major varieties, with historical and bibliographical notes.

678 LINDSAY (John). A view of the coinage of Ireland from the invasion of the Danes to the reign of George IV; with some account of the ring money; also, copious tables, lists, and descriptions of Hiberno-Danish and Irish coins, and an account of some of the principal hoards or parcels of coins discovered in Ireland. Illustrated with engravings of . . . unpublished coins. Pp [6], iv, 144; 14 plates. Cork: Luke H. Bolster, 1839.

679 NOLAN (Patrick). A monetary history of Ireland. 2 vols. London: P. S. King, 1926-8.

Pt ii. *From the Anglo-Norman invasion to the death of Elizabeth.* Pp xl, 213. Mainly a reprint of articles in *I.E.R.*, 5th ser., xvii (1921)-xix (1922).

680 O'SULLIVAN (William). The earliest Anglo-Irish coinage. Pp viii, 88; 10 plates. Dublin: Stationery Office, 1964.

At head of title: An Roinn Oideachais, Ard-Mhúsaem na h-Éireann, National Museum of Ireland.
A definitive study *c.*1182-1210.

681 SIMON (James). An essay towards an historical account of Irish coins, and of the currency of foregin [*sic*] monies in Ireland. With an appendix containing several statutes, proclamations, patents, acts of state, and letters relating to the same. Pp xv, 184; 8 plates. Dublin: printed by S. Powell for the author, 1749; 2nd ed. *as* Simon's essay on Irish coins and of the currency of foreign monies in Ireland. With Mr Snelling's Supplement; also, an additional plate . . . . 2 vols in 1. Dublin: printed for the editors by G. A. Procter, 1810.

2nd ed. is a reprint of the 1st ed. and Supplement (see **682**), with 4 extra pages and plate. A pioneer study of lasting importance.

682 SNELLING (Thomas). A supplement to Mr Simon's Essay on Irish coins. Pp 8; 3 plates. London, [1776].

Reprinted 1810, bound with 2nd ed. of Simon's *Essay* (see **681**), where the date of 1st ed. is given by W. Holmes as 1767. But see M. Dolley, 'A Snelling non-bicentenary', in *Spink's Numismatic Circular*, 1967, p 201.

XVI SEALS

683 ARMSTRONG (Edmund Clarence Richard). Descriptions of some Irish seals. In *R.S.A.I. Jn.*, xlv (1915), 143-8.
Miscellaneous, but mainly medieval. 3 plates.

684 ARMSTRONG (Edmund Clarence Richard). Irish seal-matrices and seals. Pp xii, 135. Dublin: Hodges, Figgis, 1913.
A well-illustrated, general account, including corrected editions of papers previously published elsewhere. Most of the examples described are in the R.I.A. collection.

685 ARMSTRONG (Edmund Clarence Richard). Matrices of Irish seals. In *R.I.A. Proc.*, xxx (1912-13), C, no. 20 (1913), 451-76.
Includes descriptions of several medieval examples. 4 plates.

686 BIRCH (Walter de Gray). Catalogue of seals in the Department of Manuscripts in the British Museum. 6 vols. London: Trustees of the British Museum, 1887-1900.
'Ireland' in vol. iv, pp 695-732, and plate xii.

687 CAULFIELD (Richard). Sigilla ecclesiae hibernicae illustrata: the episcopal and capitular seals of the Irish cathedral churches illustrated. Pt 1. Cashel and Emly. Pp 48. Cork: privately printed by H. Ridings, 1853.
General explanatory comments, with a detailed description of each seal. 8 plates.

688 CURTIS (Edmund). Some medieval seals out of the Ormond archives. In *R.S.A.I. Jn.*, lxvi (1936), 1-8.
Describes some typical Irish seals, 12th-16th century, especially valuable in the absence of any comprehensive work on the subject. 4 pages of plates. See also **689**.

689 CURTIS (Edmund). Some further medieval seals out of the Ormond archives, including that of Donal Reagh MacMurrough Kavanagh, King of Leinster. In *R.S.A.I. Jn.*, lxvii (1937), 72-6.
Mainly ecclesiastical. 4 plates. Supplementary to **688**.

690 JENKINSON (*Sir* Hilary). The Great Seal of England: deputed or departmental seals. In *Archaeologia*, lxxxv (1936), 293-340.
Includes 'Seals for Ireland' (pp 314-23; 4 plates), tracing the development of the Irish Great Seal during the medieval and early modern periods. Subsidiary seals are treated in less detail, owing to scanty evidence. Cf. Sir Henry C. Maxwell-Lyte, *Historical notes on the use of the Great Seal of England* (London: H.M.S.O., 1926).

691 STRICKLAND (Walter George). The ancient official seals of the City of Dublin. In *R.S.A.I. Jn.*, liii (1923), 121-32.
Description and history of medieval and later seals. 2 plates.

XVII GENEALOGY

(a) GENERAL

692 BROOKS (Eric St John). Anglo-Irish mediaeval genealogy. In *Ir. Geneal.*, ii (1943-55), 34-9.

> A survey of the English and Welsh origins of some of the early Anglo-Norman settlers.

693 BURKE (*Sir* John Bernard). A genealogical and heraldic history of the landed gentry of Ireland. 9th ed. edited by A. P. Burke. With supplement. Pp liv, 495. London: Harrison, 1899; 10th ed. Pp [6], 673. 1904; New ed., revised by A. C. Fox-Davies. Pp iv, 786. 1912; 4th [i.e. 12th] ed., edited by L. G. Pine. Pp xxxvi, 778. London: Burke's Peerage, 1958.

> 1st-9th editions published in *A genealogical and heraldic history of Great Britain and Ireland:* 1st ed., by John Burke (4 vols, London: Henry Colburn, 1833-8); 2nd ed., by John Burke and J. B. Burke (3 vols, London: Henry Colburn, 1843-9); 3rd ed., by J. B. Burke (3 vols, London: Henry Colburn, 1847-52; *repr.* London: Harrison, 1855-8); 4th-9th editions, by J. B. Burke (each in 2 vols, London: Harrison, 1862-98). 8th and 9th editions revised by Ashworth P. Burke.

694 CLARE (Wallace George). A simple guide to Irish genealogy. Pp 36. Bletchley: the author, 1937; 2nd ed. Pp 35. London: Geo. E. J. Coldwell, 1938; 3rd ed., revised by Rosemary ffolliott. Pp 45. London: Irish Genealogical Research Society, 1966.

> Describes sources of information for the compilation of an Irish pedigree, but not very useful for the middle ages. Bibliography of family histories, and a list of reference works and printed sources.

695 COKAYNE (George Edward). The complete peerage of England, Scotland, Ireland, Great Britain, and the United Kingdom, extant, extinct or dormant, alphabetically arranged and edited by G.E.C. 8 vols. London: Bell, 1887-98; New ed. revised and much enlarged by Vicary Gibbs [and others]. 13 vols. London: St Catherine P., 1910-59.

> 1st ed., vols ii-viii also published Exeter: W. Pollard.

696 DUNLEVY (M.). The medical families of mediaeval Ireland. In *What's past is prologue* (1952), pp 15-22.

> A study of Irish physicians and their writings, based largely on references in *Annals of the Kingdom of Ireland, by the Four Masters,* ed. John O'Donovan (7 vols, Dublin: Hodges & Smith, 1848-51; 2nd ed., 1856).

697 FALLEY (Margaret Dickson). Irish and Scotch-Irish ancestral research: a guide to the genealogical records, methods and sources in Ireland. 2 vols. Evanston, Ill.: the author, 1962.
Printed by Shenandoah Publishing House, Strasburg, Va.
An essential reference work for the Irish genealogist. Vol. i lists the various libraries and other repositories, describing the genealogical records they contain. Vol. ii is a bibliography of relevant works, including a family index to articles in Irish periodicals; it lists published records, unpublished family records, published sources, microfilms.

698 KIMBER (Edward). The peerage of Ireland: a genealogical and historical account of all the peers of that kingdom, their descents, collateral branches, births, marriages and issue . . . , with paternal coats of arms, crests, supporters, and mottoes . . . ; also complete list of the baronets, extinct peers, and chief governors of Ireland; some account of the antient kings, &c. . . . 2 vols. London: printed for J. Almon, 1768.
Published anonymously. Plates contain 141 coats of arms copied from J. Lodge, **699**.

699 LODGE (John). The peerage of Ireland; or, A genealogical history of the present nobility of that kingdom; with their paternal coats of arms. 4 vols. London, 1754; 2nd ed., revised, enlarged and continued by M. Archdall. 7 vols. London: G. G. J. & J. Robinson; Dublin: J. Moore, 1789.

700 MacLYSAGHT (Edward). Guide to Irish families. Pp 248. Dublin: Helicon P., 1964.
An epitome of his three major volumes, **701**, forming an alphabetical index to them. Introduction on surnames in Ireland. Bibliography of Irish family histories.

701 MacLYSAGHT (Edward). Irish families: their names, arms and origins. Illustrated by Myra Maguire. Pp 366. Dublin: Hodges, Figgis, 1957.—More Irish families. Pp 320. Galway, Dublin: O'Gorman, 1960.—Supplement to Irish families. Pp 163. Dublin: Helicon P., 1964.
Short historical accounts of individual families, covering 2,500 surnames. Maps show location of medieval septs and Norman families. 27 plates of family arms in vol. i. *Supplement* includes corrections to earlier vols. For index, see **700**.

702 MacLYSAGHT (Edward). The surnames of Ireland. Pp 252. Shannon: Irish U.P., 1969.
Alphabetical list of *c*.4,000 Gaelic, Norman and Anglo-Irish surnames, giving historical background, linguistic derivation, and location, with cross-references to his other works, **701**. Bibliography; map.

703 O'REILLY (John J.). Irish genealogy and the Public Record Office, London. In *Ir. Geneal.*, i (1937-42), 76-88.
A descriptive list of relevant records.

(b) INDIVIDUAL FAMILIES

Only a selection of the more important items is given here. For other families see bibliographies in **694, 697, 700-702.**

704 BLACKALL (*Sir* Henry William Butler). The Butlers of County Clare. In *N. Munster Antiq. Jn.*, vi (1949-52), 108-29; vii (1953-57), no. 1 (1953), 153-67; no. 2 (1955), 19-45.

705 BLACKALL (*Sir* Henry William Butler). The Galweys of Munster. In *Cork Hist. Soc. Jn.*, lxxi (1966), 138-58; lxii (1967), 20-51, 122-34; lxiii (1968), 161-74; lxiv (1969), 71-83.

706 BROOKS (Eric St John). The de Ridelisfords. In *R.S.A.I. Jn.*, lxxxi (1951), 115-38; lxxxii (1952), 45-61.
   Identifies the original family estates in Ireland, and traces their sub-infeudation and devolution.

706a BROOKS (Eric St John). The early Irish Comyns. In *R.S.A.I. Jn.*, lxxxvi (1956), 170-86.

707 BROOKS (Eric St John). The family of Marisco. In *R.S.A.I. Jn.*, lxi (1931), 22-38, 89-112; lxii (1932), 50-74.

708 BROOKS (Eric St John). The grant of Castleknock to Hugh Tyrel. In *R.S.A.I. Jn.*, lxiii (1933), 206-220.—The Tyrels of Castleknock. In *R.S.A.I. Jn.*, lxxvi (1946), 151-4.
   First part includes a supplementary note by Charles McNeill, pp 219-20.

709 BUTLER (William Francis Thomas). The pedigree and succession of the house of Mac Carthy Mór, with a map. In *R.S.A.I. Jn.*, li (1921), 32-48.
   Genealogical table. See also Samuel Trant McCarthy. *The Mac Carthys of Munster: the story of a great Irish sept* (pp 399, Dundalk: Dundalgan P., 1922).

710 CALLANAN (Martin). The de Burgos or Bourkes of Ileagh. In *N. Munster Antiq. Jn.*, i (1936-39), 67-77.

711 CAULFIELD (Richard). [Notices on the de Cogans.] In *Cork Hist. Soc. Jn.*, x (1904), 186-90.
   Extracted from the unpublished transactions of the Cork Cuvierian and Archaeological Society, 1867-8.

712 CURTIS (Edmund). The MacQuillan or Mandeville lords of the Route. In *R.I.A. Proc.*, xliv (1937-8), C, no. 4 (1938), 99-113.
   A short history of the family from the early 13th to the 17th centuries.

713 FITZGERALD (Brian). The Geraldines: an experiment in Irish government, 1169-1601. Pp 322. London, New York: Staples P., 1951.
A history of the Fitzgerald family in Ireland.

714 MATHEWS (Thomas). The O'Neills of Ulster: their history and genealogy. With illustrations, some notices of the northern septs, and an introduction by Francis Joseph Bigger. 3 vols. Dublin: Sealy, Bryers & Walker, 1907.
Vol. ii covers 1166-1519. See *R.S.A.I. Jn.*, xxxviii (1908), 403-4.

715 NICHOLLS (Kenneth William). The Fitzmaurices of Kerry. In *Kerry Arch. Soc. Jn.*, iii (1970), 23-42.
Includes correction of detail in G. H. Orpen, 'The origin of the Fitz-Maurices, barons of Kerry and Lixnaw' in *E.H.R.*, xxix (1914), 302-15 and in *Geneal. Mag.*, i (1925), 9-14, 34-7, 69-70, and in *Ireland under the Normans*, **209**, iii, p 146.

716 ORPEN (Goddard Henry). The FitzGeralds, barons of Offaly. In *R.S.A.I. Jn.*, xliv (1914), 99-113.
A detailed examination of the pedigree, correcting a number of earlier references. Genealogical table, *ante* 1176-1316. See also **713**.

717 ORPEN (Goddard Henry). Notes on the Bermingham pedigree. In *Galway Arch. Soc. Jn.*, ix (1915-16), 195-205.
An account of the family in Ireland from the Anglo-Norman invasion to c.1350. See also H. T. Knox, 'The Bermingham family of Athenry' in *Galway Arch. Soc. Jn.*, x (1917-18), 139-54, which contains a genealogical table based on Orpen's article.

718 RYAN (John). The O'Briens in Munster after Clontarf. In *N. Munster Antiq. Jn.*, ii (1940-41), 141-52; iii (1942-3), 1-52.

719 SYNOTT (Nicholas Joseph). Notes on the family of de Lacy in Ireland. In *R.S.A.I. Jn.*, xlix (1919), 113-31.

XVIII HERALDRY

720 ARMSTRONG (Edmund Clarence Richard). A note as to the time heraldry was adopted by the Irish chiefs. In *R.S.A.I. Jn.*, xliii (1913), 66-72.

Examines the evidence of the Anglo-Norman period.

721 DYKES (David Wilmur). The Anglo-Irish coinage and the ancient arms of Ireland. In *R.S.A.I. Jn.*, xcvi (1966), 111-20.

An analysis of the heraldic designs and legends on 15th and early 16th century coins.

INDEX

Aalen, F. H. A., 'The evolution of the traditional house in western Ireland' **645**
  'The origin of enclosures in eastern Ireland' **548**
Abbott, T. K., *Catalogue of the Irish manuscripts in the Library of Trinity College, Dublin* **13**
  Catalogue of the manuscripts in the Library of Trinity College, Dublin **13**
Administration **341-58**
  central **359-71**
  ecclesiastical **402-19**
  local **372-86**
Adrian IV, *see* Hadrian IV
Advowsons **407**
Agriculture **134, 135, 548-61**
Air photography **654, 670**
Alemand, L., *Histoire monastique d'Irlande* **429**
  The monastical history of Ireland **429**
  Monasticon Hibernicum **429**
Alen, John, *Register* **378**
Alphabetical index to the townlands and towns of Ireland **152**
Altschul, M., *A baronial family in medieval England* **372**
American Committee for Irish Studies, *Annual Report* **1**
Analecta Hibernica **54**
Ancient Monuments Advisory Council for Northern Ireland, *A preliminary survey of the ancient monuments of Northern Ireland* **651**
Ancient monuments of Northern Ireland **664, 665**
Andrews, J. H. **189**
  ' "Ireland in maps": a bibliographical postscript' **173**
  Ireland in maps: an introduction **172**
Andrews, M. C., 'The map of Ireland, A.D. 1300-1700' **174**
Andrews collection **174**
Anglo-Irish literature **587-94**
Anglo-Irish relations, political **311**
  social **533-47**
Anglo-Norman invasion **194, 214-46**
Anglo-Norman settlement **214-46, 441**
'Annual Report from the American Committee for Irish Studies' **1**
Annual Report of the Commissioners of Public Works in Ireland **655**
'Annual Report of the Irish Committee of Historical Sciences' **2**
Antiquities, *see* Monuments, ancient
Archaeological survey of County Down **652**
Archaeological Survey of Northern Ireland **652**
Archaeology **467, 650-71**

Archdall, M. **699**
  Monasticon Hibernicum **430**
Architecture **616, 617**
  domestic **630, 645-50**
  ecclesiastical **618-26, 657**
  military **627-44**
Archivium Hibernicum **55**
Ardagh and Clonmacnoise Antiquarian Society, *Journal* **86**
Ardee, barony **143**
Armagh, county **219**
  ecclesiastical province **390**
Armagh Diocesan Historical Society, *Seanchas Ardmhacha* **112**
Armagh Public Library **39**
Armies **259, 260, 305, 335**
Armitage, E. S. **642**
Armstrong, E. C. R., 'Descriptions of some Irish seals' **683**
  Irish seal matrices and seals **684**
  'Matrices of Irish seals' **685**
  'A note as to the time heraldry was adopted by the Irish chiefs' **720**
Armstrong, O. G., *Edward Bruce's invasion of Ireland* **279**
  'Manuscripts of the "Modus tenendi parliamentum" in the Library of Trinity College, Dublin' **341**
Arnold, B., *A concise history of Irish art* **603**
Arroasians **438, 445**
Art **603-15**
Arthurs, J. B., *Bulletin of the Ulster Place-name Society* **150**
  'Place-names' **149**
Assisi **56**
Association for the Preservation of the Memorials of the Dead, *Journal* **92**
Athlone, priory **478**
Athlone Society, *see* Old Athlone Society
Atlases, *see* Maps
Augustinians **434, 437-45**
Austin friars, *see* Augustinians
Axe, gallóglach **328**

Backmund, N., *Monasticon Praemonstratense* **439**
Baginbun, battle of **231, 232**
Bailiffs, Dublin **562**
Ball, F. E., *The judges in Ireland* **367**
Bankers **268-71**
Barberini manuscripts **313**
Barbour, John **280**
Bards **580-6**
Baronies **131, 143**
  indexes **151-4, 161**
  maps **186-8**